For Gwen Ward,
one of my favorite
promakers

— John Weld

Feb. 4, 1989

Young Man in Paris

Young Man in Paris

by

John Weld

Illustrations by Jeremy Blatchley

Academy Chicago Publishers

To my wife, Kathy,
with all the concomitants of love

Published in 1985 by
Academy Chicago, Publishers
425 N. Michigan Ave.
Chicago, IL 60611

Library of Congress Cataloging in Publication Data

Weld, John, 1905—
    Young man in Paris.

    1. Weld, John, 1905—   —Biography—Youth.
2. Authors, American—20th century—Biography.
3. Americans—France—Paris—Biography.   4. Paris
(France)—Intellectual life—20th century.   I. Title.
PS3545.E5155Z475   1984   813'.54 [B]   84-16737
ISBN 0-89733-111-7

Contents

I

Paris, the Herald, James Joyce and Others

In 1926 aspiring young writers were strongly influenced by Ernest Hemingway's *The Sun Also Rises.* Wandering through Europe, living on free love and wine. . . What could be a more perfect existence? The American intelligentsia took the position that the United States was a tasteless, materialistic, boor-filled country where artistic endeavor was stifled. Sophisticated people went abroad, or had been abroad, or were going abroad: debutantes were being 'received' by the Queen of England, rich American mothers and widows were looking for titled sons-in-law or husbands. . . . Everyone who was anyone went to Europe.

Henry Stansbury and I were no exceptions. We both worked as cub reporters on the *New York American* and shared a small basement apartment on West Ninth Street, just off Fifth Avenue. We were both twenty-one, and in 1926 had been working at the *American* for a year. We were ready to go to Europe and work on novels. We also thought that with a year's experience we were ready to become foreign correspondents. Hank's father was the head of Hearst's International News Service in Europe. His office was in London, and we both thought that he would probably be willing to give us jobs there, if we needed them.

We made plans to sail on a Belgian freighter bound for Antwerp. The day before we left, Charles Lindbergh announced that he was going to enter the great air race: a wealthy Franco-American hotel owner named Raymond B Orteig had offered a prize of $25,000 for the first non-stop air flight from New York to Paris. I had been covering this race. The weather had been unsettled that spring. Admiral Richard E. Byrd and his crew with one plane and Clarence Chamberlain and crew with another plane were at Roosevelt Field on Long Island waiting for the weather to clear so that they could take off. When Lindbergh, a tall, skinny man whom nobody had ever heard of, announced that he intended to fly alone, everybody decided that he must have lost his marbles.

We set off on our own trip and were half-way across the Atlantic when our captain received a wireless message informing him that Lindbergh had taken off in an attempt to fly to Paris by the Great Circle route, and asking all ships along his course to watch for his plane. After that we all spent a lot of time craning our necks looking at the sky.

Hank and I reached Paris a few days after The Lone Eagle had landed at Le Bourget airport; by then of course Lindbergh madness was at its height. Overnight he had become a legend. It seems to me now that he was a classic example of the truth of the maxim which tells you to be very careful when you decide what you want because you are likely to get it. Lindbergh had risked his life against great odds to gain fame and fortune, and fame came to him with a violence that smothered reality.

There was an almost insatiable demand for information about him. No detail was too insignificant for the public. Thanks to Hank's father, Hank and I were hired as reporters for International News Service to cover the great man, who was staying at the U.S. Embassy in Paris as the guest of the Ambassador, Myron T. Herrick. We were told to report what he ate, what kind of sleeping garment he preferred, how he liked his eggs, and whether he drank coffee, and if he did, what if anything he put in it. I was assigned to follow him and note down every word he said for posterity. Most of what he said was commonplace and platitudinous, but dutifully I wrote it all down.

The job lasted until Lindbergh returned to New York. Hank and I couldn't find anything else to do in Paris, so we took the money we had earned and went to work on our novels at Le Touquet-Paris Plage, a resort on the English Channel. We stayed in a pension called Le Beau Soleil.

We didn't get much writing done there, but we did do a spectacular job of sowing our seed. Mlle Georgette, the landlady, was a plump woman of about forty, with hennaed hair. When our money ran out, she allowed us to work out our board in her bed.

Hank and I had once before had a maison à trois in New York. We had only one double bed in our basement apartment so whenever one of us needed the place the other would go out. One night Hank came home with a small dark girl he had met in Barney Gallant's speakeasy. I left and stayed out until I was exhausted, but when I got home the girl was still there. In fact both of them were asleep, so I got into bed with them. She stayed for six weeks. Her name was Martha, but we did not think that suited her, so we called her Juliana. She had come to New York from some place in the Middle West—I think it was Sioux City—and she had run out of money, so she had no place to go. She wanted to be an artist. The three of us settled down cozily; she did the housework and cooking and shared her favors equally with the two of us. We three became very close, and there was no jealousy between Hank and me. Indeed, we both considered the arrangement idyllic. Then one morning it ended abruptly. Juliana got up and cooked breakfast for us and then, just as we were leaving for work, told us that she was going to be married at noon to one of our friends, a United Press reporter. We never saw her again.

But Mlle Georgette was far more innovative and imaginative than Martha-Juliana had been. She needed both Hank and me; one man was really not enough for her. We performed incredible gymnastics. I had had numerous sexual fantasies, but I have never been able to fantasize such a variety of sexual aberrations. It was more of a contest than a collaboration. Young as we were, we could not go the distance to her satisfaction.

And Georgette was not the only woman in her establishment. At that time it was the custom for Frenchmen to send their wives or mistresses to the seashore to give themselves a little rest. Consequently the hotel was alive with young and pretty women, almost all of them receptive. No sooner did an attractive woman depart than another came to take her bed. Hank and I could really not accommodate them all. But we gave it the old college try. We leaned into it with everything we had, but it was a losing battle. Our survival that summer was a noteworthy achievement, like floating over Niagara Falls in a barrel.

We stayed on for a year at the pension Le Beau Soleil.

Despite our energetic activities we were still able to trudge through the dunes, study French and write the odd paragraph. The only flaw in this paradise was a more and more noticeable lack of money. I did get one bonanza: a check for three hundred dollars from *Colliers Weekly* for an article about my experiences as a Hollywood stunt man. For once I was able to pay off our creditors.

As our second summer at Paris-Plage was drawing to a close, I was offered a job at the Paris *Herald.* I was enjoying my romantic existence, but I could not afford to turn down the opportunity to make some money and further my career. So I set out for Paris, leaving Hank behind to look after Mlle Georgette, which he did until he became sufficiently drained to borrow some money from his father and return home.

Although I put off writing fiction so that I could act the playboy, I never put off writing to my mother. She was a practising astrologer in New York, and contributed a monthly article on foreign affairs to *American Astrology* magazine. I had not lived with her since I was eleven, when she had sent me, for my health, to a Colorado ranch. After that I had lived at military schools and then at Auburn University in Alabama. But she was my anchor in this wobbly world, and we wrote faithfully to each other until her death. Fortunately she kept all of my letters, so that I was able to draw on them for much of this book.

I have moved into a tiny apartment on the rue Delambre just behind Le Café Dôme. It's on the fifth floor and there is no elevator. It is advertised as 'conforte moderne', which means that it is supposed to include steam heating (there is very little; one dresses warmly even when going to bed), electricity, a bath and a toilet. I do have electric light, though it some-times goes off, but the one bath is for the six of us who live on this floor. The toilet too is well removed from me. It is not a porcelain seat but an enamel-bordered hole in the floor with footrests on either side. A water tank with a metal chain hanging from it is on the wall above. This contraption is known for some reason as a Turkish. One has to take one's own toilet paper and I discovered that before pulling the chain it is wise to move as far as possible from the hole. Then a quick tug, making sure that the chain doesn't take the skin off your hand—and run like hell.

The grocery store here (epicerie), unlike those at home, does not sell fresh vegetables, meat or dairy products. There are vegetable shops, and some butcher shops—which have distinctive red and white awnings—sell only beef and lamb. Others sell only pork and horsemeat. And you can buy chickens at the dairy shop, along with milk, cheese and butter. Incidentally, the cheaper restaurants serve a thing called Belgian paté, which is a mixture of rabbit and horsemeat. Elliot Paul says the paté is "one horse and one rabbit."

The ex-wife of Hendrik Willem van Loon lives in this building, and our cleaning woman also works for e.e. cummings. I have always been in awe of celebrities, so discovering these things made me feel pretty important when I moved in. After I unpacked, I went right over to Le Dôme to have a drink. It is the most famous and popular bistro on the Left Bank, the favorite well of artists and would-be artists of all kinds. I was lucky to find a place on the terrace, since it is crowded day and night. Sitting there, I felt sud-denly mature—new house, new job and—to me at least—new world.

You know that I have wanted to be a writer ever since you got that piece of doggerel I wrote published in the *Birmingham Age-Herald* when I was seven. I was hooked then, once I saw my name in print. Now that I am twenty-two I am still hooked, and I am going to apply myself. I will work on the *Herald* to earn a living, and work in my spare time on a book to earn fame.

I am living in the heart of Bohemia. It's called the Latin Quarter, I don't know why. Famous people have indulged themselves here, in art and sin. The Boulevard Montparnasse cuts through the Quarter: up there is La Closerie des Lilas, where Svengali took Trilby, and across the carrefour, where it intersects with the Boulevard Raspail, is the Rotunda, another famous cafe. On that first visit to the Dôme I saw an Oriental man a couple of tables away, with black bangs and gold-rimmed glasses. I learned later that he is the celebrated Japanese artist Foujita.

The Dôme became my sitting room, dining room and bar—as familiar to me as the *Herald* offices. I almost always had breakfast there—coffee and a croissant—and frequently stopped in for a nightcap after a long day. Naturally I got to know a number of habitués. Among the well-known ones were Kiki, an artist's model who carried a white mouse on her arm; Raymond Duncan, Isadora's brother, who always wore a Grecian robe and sandals; Gertrude Stein and Alice Toklas; Jacques Lipschitz, the big, tousled, energetic sculptor; Ford Madox Ford, Ludwig Lewisohn and Ezra Pound, all rising writers at the time who were all kindly willing at times to discuss the art of story-telling with me. Pound was the personification of a poet, with a golden beard, open shirt and long, curly hair: he was also a non-stop talker who could pon-

Ezra Pound

tificate his listeners to sleep. Others who came occasionally were George Antheil, Robert MacAlmon, Ethel Moorehead and Ernest Walsh. Moorehead and Walsh published *This Quarter,* a literary magazine to which, eventually, I contributed some stories.

There were many young intellectuals in the Dôme circle at that time, all producing avant-garde works—novels without punctuation, poems in strange languages, electric operas. Many of us considered them poseurs, self-conscious juveniles trying to revolutionize the literary world.

James Joyce sometimes came to the Dôme, usually with his maternal Irish wife. He was slight, handsome, wore a small Van Dyke beard, and seemed unusually timid, shrinking from contact with even ardent admirers. He would not grant interviews, and it was difficult, even in ordinary conversation, to get him to talk about himself. I sat with him whenever I could, and in time he became comfortable with me. He lived with his wife, son and daughter near the Champ-de-Mars; sometimes his friends gathered in his apartment there. He was a charming host with a strong sense of humor; with the help of a little wine he became something of a show-off. He used to say jokingly that he and John McCormack had learned music together. Mrs Joyce was a motherly sort of woman who did not pretend to understand the things her husband wrote.

Since Joyce was nearly blind, he asked me one day if I would type a letter for him. I did it gladly, and typed several others for him from time to time. I could not make much of his work—particularly *Work in Progress,* which became *Finnegan's Wake*—but his letters were clear enough. He believed himself to be—and perhaps was—the hardest-working writer of all time. He told Elliot

The author with James Joyce

Paul that twenty pages of his *Work in Progress,* which was printed in *transition,* had taken him 1200 hours of work. I learned a lot of things from Joyce, not the least of which was persistence.

Joyce liked to talk about women, and to contrast what he saw as their generosity, thoughtfulness and kindness with the egotism, selfishness, despotism and fault-finding of men.

"Women will give you the shirts off their backs, and gladly," he said. "Consider my wife. She continually amazes me. Day after day she looks after me, she takes care of me. She is always worrying about my health, about my eyesight, my work, my happiness. She plans our meals, and cooks them well; she does laundry and ironing, mends, dusts, lays fires, washes windows, goes marketing, and protects me from strangers. She even keeps the books and pays the bills. And she does it all without pay.

"And I sit at my desk and write. She sees me as an artist, she thinks I need time to create. Probably no one will publish my work, and only she may read it, and if she does read it, the chances are good that she won't understand it. But she believes strongly in my talent, and she wants me to have time to write. Can you imagine a man being so unselfish?

"All I can do for her is praise her and thank her for everything she does. I believe that nothing is so rewarding as praise—one should always give kudos when they are due. I think that laudation, admiration—even adoration—are the cements and oils of love and marriage. They keep the wheels greased and turning. A little flattery doesn't hurt either."

I went to work for the Paris *Herald* in 1928 in a dingy building on the rue de Louvre, in the midst of Les Halles, the great central market, which Emile Zola called "the belly of Paris". About midnight, when the paper was put to bed, hundreds of people were in the streets, pushing carts with innumerable crates of fruits, vegetables, meat, fish and fowl brought in from the countryside and the sea for the million meals of the coming day. It was a picturesque and romantic setting for a newspaper shop—one of the oldest parts of a very old city.

The paper had been founded in 1887 by James Gordon Bennett, Jr, who had come to live in France after a humiliating series of events which began on New Year's Day in 1877 when he went in an inebriated condition to visit his prospective fiancée, Caroline May. Caroline's brother Frederick took exception to what he considered Bennett's ungentlemanly behavior and two days later horsewhipped him in front of the Union Club on Fifth Avenue. Bennett challenged May to a duel: both of them missed. Bennett felt so humiliated that he became a permanent expatriate. His flamboyant personality kept him in the public eye: he hobnobbed with royalty, bought an estate at Versailles, a mansion on the Riviera, a huge house in Paris, a castle in Scotland and a yacht that cost over 600,000 pre-World War I dollars. He was so eccentric that when he heard that Frederick May was coming to Paris, he took to wearing a coat of mail under his conventional clothing. He was supposed to have driven a tallyho stark naked through the streets of Paris. Once he went berserk at Maxim's, jerking tablecloths off tables at which diners were sitting, smashing the crystal and china, and attempting to dance on the considerable debris. He paid several thousand dollars in damages for this escapade.

After he had controlled his successful *New York Herald* for ten years from France, he decided to publish a newspaper in Paris and hired a small staff, mostly English. He said to them, "I want you gentlemen to remember that I am the only reader of this paper. I am the only one to be pleased. If I want the columns turned upside down, they must be turned upside down. I consider a dead dog in the rue de Louvre more interesting for the *Herald* than a devastating flood in China. I want one feature article a day. If I say the feature is to be black beetles, black beetles it's going to be."

The Paris paper was a toy for him, a kind of hobby to engage his energies. He enjoyed it; he didn't expect it to make money, and indeed it is estimated that in the early years it lost as much as $100,000 a year. He received news by cable from New York and London and from the *New York Herald* correspondents around the world. Thus the *Herald* was able to provide more news than any other newspaper in France. The French press unashamedly borrowed items from it. After the turn of the century, the number of American tourists in France rose considerably, and the paper gained in reputation and circulation. The early years of the century were the heydey of royalty: titled people frequented the expensive playgrounds— Carlsbad, Aix-les-Bains, St Moritz, Marienbad and so on—and the *Herald* faithfully recounted gossip about them. All the royal houses of Europe had subscriptions to the paper, or were given complimentary copies. Two hundred copies went daily to the Czar of all the Russias.

In 1914 when the Germans advanced on Paris, thousands fled the capital, and all the newspapers shut down . . . except the *Herald,* which did not miss a single issue. Bennett, who was 73 at the time, stayed at work in Paris. On the first day of mobilization the paper had to be gotten out by a skeleton staff: two printers, one stereotyper and three men in the composing room. Throughout the war Bennett continued payment of full salaries to the wives of employees who had enlisted in the armed forces. When the French government fled to Bordeaux, Bennett stayed on, boosting French morale by damning the Boche in strong editorials during Zeppelin raids and attacks by Big Bertha, the German canon. Sometimes he could get only enough paper to print one sheet, in English on one side and French on the other. The police often had to disperse crowds gathered before the *Herald's* bulletin board, which was the only source of immediate news in the city. It was from the *Herald* that the world learned that Galleni's taxicab army had turned back the Germans from the gates of Paris.

When the United States entered the war, Bennett had only about a year to live. He did not see the Armistice, but died on May 15, 1918, five days after his seventy-seventh birthday.

During my time the paper was written and edited by some bizarre characters—expatriates, wanderers, iconoclasts, romantics. Elliot Paul edited the correspondence columns, which were considered an important feature. Often he wrote the letters himself, making up signatures, and he encouraged his confreres to do likewise. Elliot also provided column fillers, like "Why do European people eat mussels?" The answer was printed upside down at the bottom of the column. „because mussels are good to eat." On his day off, about once a week, he vanished, presumably into a bordello, since bordellos were his hobby. Once he vanished from the office for an entire week, and we all thought he was dead. But he finally turned up. "Been doig research," was all he would tell us.

He did not cut a romantic figure: he was short and stout, wore a Van Dyke beard, and his sparse hair was plastered carefully across his scalp. But when I met him he had already had three wives, each progressively richer. Eventually he was to marry for a fourth time. He said he married rich women because he needed the money. Most of his motivations were uncomplicated, and so were his emotional reactions.

We became friends. I admired him; I thought he was a major talent. I don't know what he saw in me: perhaps he just wanted an admirer. From him I learned to peel away preconceptions and evaluate, as far as possible, without prejudice. He said there was virtue in sin, good in evil, and beauty in ugliness. He seemed to be able to see through poses of all kinds, and I tried to imitate him, in that and other ways.

Elliot with Eugene Jolas, had been one of the founders and editors of *transition*, the avant-garde magazine. It was typical of young intellectuals of the time that the title of the magazine should be written in lower-case letters. *transition* printed some early poetry of e.e. cummings', much by Gertrude Stein, and a lot of Joyce's *Work in Progress,* which was regarded then as his master-piece. I was not alone in considering it a mass of gibber-ish, but Elliot said that it gave a multitudinous account of the development of civilization and the history of man-kind, and that it dramatized original sin, the Fall and the Redemption. He told me that to understand it, one had to spend as much time reading it as Joyce had spent writing it. Knowing Elliot, I am pretty sure he and Jolas started to print Joyce as a kind of lark. Ditto Gertrude Stein. When *transition* published Stein's *Essay on Composition as Ex-planation,* Elliot mixed up the pages of the manuscript. Miss Stein protested vehemently, and the piece had to be republished as she had written it. Elliot told me that Stein was the only person who commented; no other reader seemed to notice.

Elliot lived in a fourth floor apartment on the rue de

la Huchette overlooking the Seine, the Ile de la Cité and Nôtre Dame. He almost loved this section of the city and wrote charmingly about it in *The Last Time I Saw Paris*. I say almost, because Elliot would not have used the word 'love' to describe his feeling for any thing, or any place; he used it only for people, mostly women. From his living room windows one could watch the sun rise over the cathedral; laden barges drifted down the south branch of the river, coming from as far away as Belgium and bound for Rouen or Le Havre. One could see also the Hotel Dieu, the city hospital, and the Palais de Justice. It was a romantic setting, and Elliot was a romantic.

As we became friendly, I began to visit him, usually to play bridge. I believe he was married at the time, although none of us was sure. In any case he was living with an American woman whose name I have forgotten. Perhaps it was Flora; he dedicated his book about Paris to her. Anyway, he had money then, because he was gener ous with food and drink. He was a connoisseur of both.

I wrote Mother about one of my evenings with the Pauls, and she wrote back saying she was upset because I seemed to be drinking too much.

It's true [I replied], I do drink a lot. It's part of the life here; everyone does it. Fortunately I have a tolerance for alcohol and rarely get ossified. But it helps me. Sober, I am likely to be awkward and obsequious, especially with famous people. After a couple of glasses of wine, my confidence increases; I become, to myself at least, amusing, charming, even brilliant. This is certainly useful in my work; it helps me to overcome my feelings of shyness and inadequacy and to ask penetrating, personal questions, as I must do, as a reporter.

The author at a sidewalk cafe

So alcohol in moderation seems to be good for me. After a little wine, I am often surprised at the clarity of my thought, the sharpness of my wit. Everything seems quite simple. But don't worry. I promise you I won't become an alcoholic.

In prompt reply, she wrote, "What you have to say about your drinking is the attitude of every sot. So be careful."

II
A Night With Sparrow
on the Town

Another memorable character on the staff of the *Herald* was Sparrow Robertson, small, lean like a jockey, and seventy-two years old when I met him. He wrote a column called "Sporting Gossip", which was precisely that: a record of his daily and nightly wanderings, the persons he met, and their chit-chat. It was the most popular feature in the paper; Sparrow was consequently a kind of mini-celebrity. He had been born in Edinburgh about 1856 and emigrated at an early age with his parents to New York where he had little schooling but worked at a number of jobs. About 1900 he opened a sporting goods store near City Hall which became a rendezvous for athletes and sportswriters. When Prohibition came into effect he sold the business and moved to Paris.

He was a heavy drinker and alcohol seemed to bring out the best in him, but oddly enough he came to France with a contingent of the YMCA. How he was able to get a job writing for the *Herald* is a story which even in the twenties was lost in the mists of history. But it was a lucky day for him and for the paper. Elliot Paul said, "The thought that he might not have been hired because he couldn't type or spell is sobering enough to close all the bars in Christendom."

His column was like a diary. He would tap it out on a battered typewriter, take it, misspelled and often illegible, to a copy editor and expect that unfortunate to decipher and correct it. Because the job was so time-consuming, the editor would pan it off on newcomers if he could. Soon after I started work the copy landed on my desk. "Don't change anything," I was told. "Just make it readable."

I had to concentrate for several minutes before I was able to understand the lead sentence not only because much of it was exed out, but because Sparrow disregarded syntax as well as spelling. Nevertheless any change in his work would bring out his rage, which could be violent. Here are some samples of his writing:

> The end of a perfect Thanksgiving Day. Early in the afternoon of Thursday I dropped into Jeff Dickson's office and he prevailed upon me to remain and hear the returns of the Royal Wedding in London. I did, and during the come-over some refreshments were offered and not refused. After, it was a case of making a call at Henry's Bar in the rue Volney, where an excellent free lunch, and drinks included, was served. It was a swell layout and it was deeply appreciated by the mass which attended.
>
> Then it was a visit to Otto's Bar, where we found the champion cocktail shaker in fine form. After an hour or two passed with Otto, it was time to make a visit to Harry's aquarium, and what a bunch we did meet there! While in old boy Harry's place I met a pal, one well known in the American, English and Cana-

dian colonies of Paris. He said, "Sparrow, come to my home tonight and we will eat cold turkey, drink White Horse and smoke nine-inch-long Havana cigars." It sounded good to me and I told our old pal that I was on.

It appears that our old pal should have been at his home at two o'clock to carve Mr. Turkey for his missus and a few guests, but he fell in (probably he was accused of) with some evil companions. He was evidently wise to the fact that he had done something wrong when he invited me to have some cold turkey with him and I was being made his alibi after his being about nine hours late for his family Thanksgiving dinner.

We left Harry's and hopped into a taxi bound for Johnny's Bar in the rue Pierre-Charron. "We need a little priming up before meeting my missus," said our old pal, "and I want to present you to mamma feeling quite jolly. What time is it now?" he asked, as we were going up in the lift to his apartment. "Eleven fifteen," said I. "I am just ten hours late for our turkey dinner," said our pal. "But better late than never." Mamma opened the door of the apartment. It was one swell looking place. "Mamma, meet Sparrow Robertson. I have brought him home to eat some cold turkey, drink some White Horse and smoke a few of my Havana cigars!" It sounded good to me, but when I took a look at mamma's eyes, I thought a getaway was the best for me, and she helped me leaving when she said, "There will be no cold turkey, and Mr. Sparrow, you had better come around some other night as there will probably be a fight in this establishment tonight."

I beat it down six flights of stairs, and believe me the laugh I got out of what our pal was in for did me just as much good as a dish of cold turkey washed

down with White Horse, and nine-inch Havana
smokes would have done. It sure did make an end of
a perfect day for me, but maybe not for our old pal!

Syd Clark, the general secretary of the TNT Club,
is taking a much needed rest at a private home, a
short distance outside of Paris. Syd and our other old
pal, Larry Darr, keeps working out in a physical way
daily with throwing the medicine ball, punching the
bag, doing a little boxing and winding up with a card
game.

This prose fascinated many people. Eugene O'Neill
lived near Tours during the Twenties and he told a drama
critic who came to interview him that he went to the
village first thing every morning to get his *Herald* because
he could not start the day until he had read Sparrow's
column.

My mother, the astrologer, believed that people lived
their lives according to the time when they were born.
Those born early in the morning became early risers;
those born after midday were inclined to live their lives at
night. That might be true; in any case, Sparrow was a
night person. His day started in the late afternoon, usually
at Harry's New York Bar on the rue Danou, and ended at
dawn or later in the Bal Taborin or some other boîtes de
nuit in Montmartre or the Place Pigalle. En route he made
a number of stops here and there for gossip and a drink
or two.

He usually travelled his beat alone, but sometimes
pals—he called every one 'old pal'—would go along part of
the way. It's a safe bet that none of them went the
distance.

After I had been on the paper a few months, I asked
Sparrow if I could come along with him one evening, and
he said yes. I was eager to learn about the celebrated

night-life on the Right Bank. On one of my days-off we
met about four o'clock in Harry's New York Bar. I got
there first, and when Sparrow entered he was greeted so
effusively in so many parts of the room that it was some
time before he saw me.

"Glad you made it, old pal," he said. "What'll you have
to drink?"

Harry McElhone was behind the bar; he owned the
joint. He was English, blond, chubby and ingratiating. He
greeted Sparrow warmly, and Sparrow introduced me.
Harry shook my hand and said he was glad to meet any
friend of Sparrow's. Then he indicated a man standing
nearby.

"Meet Pete Emerald," he said. "He's just in from New
York."

"Howdy, pal," Sparrow said, and shook Emerald's
hand. "New York's my home town."

Emerald looked as if he might be an actor, a prizefight
manager or professional gambler. He was slender, about
my height, six feet, and his eyes were gray and cold under
heavy dark brows. The skin around his eyes was dark. He
looked dissipated. He was well dressed: gray, pinstripe
suit, blue shirt and darker blue tie, gray hound's-tooth
cap. When he shook my hand he did not smile. "Howdy,"
he said.

"When'd you get in?" Sparrow asked.

"Couple days ago."

"First trip?"

"Yeh."

"By yourself?"

"Yeh."

Harry said to me, "What are you going to drink?" He
knew what Sparrow wanted: brandy. Pete Emerald was
drinking Scotch: I ordered it too.

Pete Emerald

Sparrow said to Emerald, "What's your racket?"

"Oh, I've got a little night club back home."

It turned out that Pete and Sparrow had mutual friends in the sports world; Sparrow immediately adopted him as a pal. When we left Harry's, Pete went with us to our next stop, which was at Henry's on the rue Volney, the oldest American bar in Paris. Harry's had been lively, even raucous; Henry's was sedate. Most of the patrons were dignified businessmen who gathered regularly before lunch and dinner to have a few drinks and play dominoes. They all knew Sparrow and greeted him with warmth. We stayed long enough for one drink, Sparrow made some notes and then we went on to the Hotel Chatham bar, where the racing crowd hung out. Sparrow received his usual fervent greeting, we had a drink, he made some notes and we proceeded to the Silver Ring, a bar recently opened by Jeff Dickson, one of Sparrow's close pals and sponsors.

Jeff was a Mississippi boy who had come to Paris some years before as an assistant cameraman for Pathé Movie News. When he lost that job, he began staging boxing bouts. Boxing was primarily an American sport, but the French took to it quickly, and Jeff became very successful. When I met him he was operating the Palais de Sport and the Salle Wagram, an auditorium larger than Madison Square Garden. He had become a local celebrity: a profile of him had been written for the *New Yorker* by George Rehm, the sports editor of the *Herald*. George was related to Janet Flanner, the *New Yorker's* Paris correspondent.

In most of the places Pete and I alternately bought drinks for each other, but Sparrow didn't have to spend a franc. Sometimes he would say to the patron, "How about a round for my pals?" and if a waiter brought us the bill, he would tell him to take it to his boss.

By the time we left the Silver Ring, I had three sheets to the wind and was sailing; my feet felt as though they were several inches above the pavement. Pete appeared to be holding his own and Sparrow, looking sober as the proverbial judge, said he thought it was time to "manger", so we got into a taxi and went to his favorite eating place, Luigi's, an Italian-American restaurant between the Opera and the Madeleine. It was frequented principally by Americans and English, thanks largely to the publicity generated by Sparrow. Luigi was suitably grateful. We had a sumptuous dinner at a good table and consumed two bottles of wine, all at the expense of the house.

Sparrow, acting the connoisseur, was particular about the wine. "I always have it with food," he told us. "It gives me a chance to lay off the hard stuff."

Luigi ran an all-night cabaret on the floor above the restaurant. It was there, early one morning, Sparrow told us, that he had come upon the Prince of Wales with a small party. "I walked up to His Royal Highness, shook his hand and said, 'Well, my old pal! Howdy-do?' The Prince was very cordial, so I rendered for him my favorite song, 'Mister Dooley's Geese', which pleased him very much."

[The next edition of the *Herald* included this item: "I ran into the Prince of Wales the other night in a well-known thirst emporium and gave him the low-down on the sports situation. His Highness is one of my Old Pals and one real sport."]

We sat at dinner for quite a while; our stay was pro-longed by the stream of visitors coming to say hello to Sparrow, and it was after ten when we finally left Luigi's. Our next two stops, Otto's and Johnny's, were both on the rue Pierre Charron, off the Champs Elysées. At Otto's I switched to beer. Johnny's was in the basement of a building opposite the American Legion building. When I mentioned this to Pete, he said, "I was in the Army." He didn't tell me what I was to learn later: that he had deserted.

It was crowding midnight when we got back to Harry's. The place was packed. Sparrow's arrival was greeted with intemperate shouts of gaiety and glee. It was known that it was his custom to show up there at midnight, and there were people in the crowd who were waiting to meet him. He went about, greeting pals, gathering gossip and accepting kudos and drinks, while Pete and I squeezed into tight places at the end of the bar, an eddy in the melee. I was glad to have a respite from imbibing.

We sipped coffee while we waited for our guide to free himself from his admirers. I questioned Pete about himself, but he answered mostly in monosyllables. He had been born in Brooklyn, he was married but had no children and lived on a farm in upstate New York. He did not ask me anything about myself, but he did give me his opinion of newsmen. "As a rule," he said, "I don't like them. They create characters, and if you won't live up to the character they create, the public thinks you're no good."

I thought that was an odd opinion and asked how he had arrived at it.

"Oh, my name's been in the papers. They've made an ogre out of me. People expect horns to grow out of my head. They want me to talk tough. I never said 'youse' in my life."

I guessed that he had had a brush with the law, probably because of his 'night club', which was undoubtedly a speakeasy. But I did not think I should ask him about it. The conversation died.

At about one o'clock we left. This was the beginning of the night's second round for Sparrow. Our next stop was Fred Payne's, a small roosting place for English chorus girls who performed in the music halls of the Place Pigalle. It was just behind the Church of the Trinité but it was far removed from heaven. Sparrow introduced Pete and me to the proprietor and he bought us a drink. I switched back to scotch. Payne's prices were high and the food was not very good, but what Sparrow liked about the place were the girls. They were young, pretty and extremely friendly. Five hundred francs, or twenty dollars, would buy any one of them for a night. Pete bought drinks for several of them and I think he was reluctant to leave when Sparrow announced it was time for us to go.

We went on to two cabarets, Bricktop's and Florence's, both run by black women. Bricktop's was a favorite of Sparrow's because she fed him and, when he ran out of gas—as he sometimes did at about this time—gave him a place to take a nap. The night I was with him he did not need a rest. But I did. I hd gone about as far as my strength and endurance would carry me. Daylight would find Sparrow at the Bal Taborin or one of the other boîtes de nuit, but I left him at Florence's at about four o'clock. I don't know what happened to Pete; maybe he went back to the English girls at Payne's. And I don't remember getting home.

How Sparrow managed to make this pilgrimage five nights a week and stay alive is one of the great mysteries, like the Pyramids. Maybe he got a lot of nourishment from the food he nibbled during his peregrinations and from the many scotches and bottles of wine he drank. Small as he was, he drank more without getting sozzled than anyone I ever knew. The juice of Scotland seemed to recharge his batteries. Then, too, he had the ability to take short naps at will. Sometimes after his nightly sojourns he would come back to the *Herald* and take a long

Robert McAlmon

nap in his cubicle of an office before writing his column. Whatever the reason for his durability, we all used to marvel at it.

I kept thinking about Pete Emerald. I wondered whether he was traveling under a false name, whether he was on the run because he had committed a felony, or had abandoned his wife. I saw a small item in *The New York Herald Tribune,* which always got to Paris a week late, that Jack (Legs) Diamond, the notorious gangster, was in Europe and it suddenly dawned on me that Emerald might be Diamond. I mentioned this to Eric Hawkins, the managing editor, and he thought there might be something in it. He assigned me to find out. I cabled the New York office and asked for a file on Diamond. It was several days before I received a reply.

In the meantime the office received a message from New York asking assistance for a Mrs Caleb Foster, a friend of the publisher, who was arriving on the *S.S. DeGrasse.* I was assigned the job. As it turned out it was an assignment that kept me busy.

III
A Lady in Distress

The boat train carrying the passengers from the *DeGrasse* was scheduled to arrive shortly before noon at the Gare St Lazare. I had my usual breakfast of croissant and coffee, worked on my novel for a couple of hours and then, in front of the Dôme, boarded a bus which rolled down Raspail and into Saint Germain, groaning at each turn and wheezing at each stop. As we crossed the Seine on the Pont Royal, we saw empty barges, riding high, being towed upstream; beyond was the faint outline of Notre Dame. Downriver the Eiffel Tower rose out of the trees into fog and on the right bank were the Petit and Grand Palais art galleries. In the Place de la Concorde a gendarme signalled with his white baton: the bus ground to a stop, and the cars behind it followed suit, like chicks following a hen. At another signal the bus lurched forward. I amused myself by admiring the statuary en route: stone women in various stages of undress. . . . At the rue de Rivoli the bus halted, the conductor unlatched the leather-covered chain and two giggling girls got off. They wore black cotton hose and I thought how much prettier their legs would have looked sheathed in silk.

I alighted at L'Opéra and walked down the rue Auber to the railroad station. The boat train was pulling into the shed. Some of the baggage had been unloaded and I went along the quai, rubbing shoulders with blue-shirted porters, travel agents and steamship clerks, looking at the tags. Finally I found Mrs Foster's tag on a large suitcase. I was just jotting down the Minneapolis address when she came up.

"You leave that alone, young man," she said. "Those are mine."

She was about fifty, slight, authoritative and stern. She wore a long black coat with a fur collar and a black feathered felt hat. She spoke to the porter in English. "That one and that one and the black hatbox over there. No, not that one! Yes, that. Those four."

I introduced myself.

"Oh," she said, softening slightly, "you're from the *Herald*."

"I've been asked by our publisher, Mrs Reid, to assist you."

"Well, that's just fine. I suppose you speak French?"

"Pretty well."

The porter asked, "Taxi?"

She turned to him. "Of course we want a taxi. Now let me see." She fished in her handbag. "I have to find the name of that hotel. Now what on earth did I do with it? It's where my daughter is staying. Oh, here it is." She brought forth a card and handed it to me.

"Vingt-neuf rue Cassette," I said, reading it. "Twenty-nine rue Cassette."

"I don't speak French at all," Mrs Foster said. She looked at the porter.

"Ne comprends pas l'Anglais," the porter said.

"What did he say?"

"He said he doesn't speak English."

"Oh, my!" Mrs Foster said. "What a funny place!"

"Allons." The porter strapped the four bags over his shoulders and set off toward the SORTIE sign, staggering slightly. "Attention, attention," he repeated, clearing the way. Outside a taxi pulled up at once and he put the bags in the front seat. I opened the rear door, and when Mrs Porter started to get in, the porter touched her arm. "Pardon, Madame," he said, holding out his hand, palm up.

"Oh, yes," she said and looked at me. I suggested ten francs. She brought out a sheaf of dollars and peeled one off for him. I told her that was worth twenty-five francs. "I don't have any francs," she said.

I noted with some qualms that the driver had stared at her roll of money.

"I think I'd better go with you," I said.

She greeted this suggestion with relief. "That would be nice," she said. I gave the driver the address and got in.

Once under way, Mrs Foster still seemed tense.

"Tell him not to go so fast," she said to me. I did, but I did not notice much response.

"You mentioned your daughter," I said. "How long has she been in Paris?"

"About a year," she said. Her eyes restlessly examined the passing scene. "She's divorced, you see. She wants to be an artist. Her husband is taking care of their child. I've come to take her home."

"You mean to say you had to come all the way over here to get her?"

"She doesn't answer my letters," Mrs Foster said.

She continued to look out of the window, holding her handbag tightly in her thin hands.

"Couldn't you just cut off her income?" I asked, after a pause. "She'd have to come home then."

Mrs Foster glanced at me briefly. "She has money of her own," she said. "That's the trouble. Her father left it to her. She's very extravagant; he spoiled her. She was the apple of his eye."

As we pulled up to the pension on the rue Cassette, she said in a low voice, "How much do you think I should pay him? I think he drove us all over town before he got here."

"No, he came directly. Give him two dollars."

She paid him and I helped her out of the car. A hotel porter picked up her bags and led us into the lobby. Her black hat was slightly askew; it made her look tipsy as she approached the desk.

"I'm Mrs Caleb Foster of Minneapolis. Is my daughter Hope Bell here?"

The young woman behind the desk shook her head. "Oh, no madame. Madame Bell no here any more."

The feathers trembled on the black hat. "Not here? Did you say she wasn't here? Well, where has she gone?"

The concierge took some cards from a box. "Peut-être," she said, and began to go through them. Finally she held one up. "Hôtel des Écoles, numero quinze rue Delambre."

Mrs Foster looked at me in despair. I nodded soothingly. "I know where that is," I said.

But she still clung to the desk. "How long ago did she leave?" she asked.

"Oh, more than a month, Madame." Mrs Foster sighed. "Would Madame like a room here?"

"Well. . ." She hesitated. "I guess so. I can't be running all over town looking for my daughter without a roof over my head." She turned to me, her hat slipping more askew. "I can't imagine why she didn't come to the station. I wrote her I was coming."

"Maybe she didn't get your letter. The postal service here isn't the best in the world. Lots of times mail from other countries ends up in the dead-letter bin."

"Can't we telephone her?"

"No telephone here," the concierge said. "Café down the street."

"It's not easy to telephone," I said. "It's usually quicker to send a message by hand. Phone service here isn't the way it is back home. It's particularly bad for foreigners. And when you want to call long distance you have to go to a post office and wait in line. Sometimes it takes hours."

Mrs Foster sighed again. "Well, I'll go with you then," she said. "But first I want to go to my room."

The young woman signalled the porter, who was standing over the bags, dreamily surveying the ceiling, with the stub of a cigarette between his lips. He pocketed the room key and walked across the small lobby to the elevator door. It was a cage type of elevator that could carry three adults. The porter opened the glass door and pushed back the gate. Mrs Foster began to enter and paused.

"What's that thing you've got in your mouth?" she said to the porter.

Startled, he removed the butt from his mouth and looked at it. "C'est un cigaret," he said.

"Well, throw it away. It's finished."

The porter looked at me for a moment, and then shrugged and dropped the butt into a sand-filled receptacle. He piled the bags into the elevator after Mrs Foster and squeezed himself in. "I'll wait here," I said.

The porter reappeared promptly; Mrs Foster took a

while longer. She came down the stairs. Her hair and her hat had been straightened and she looked more in command of herself. But she looked very angry.

"Whatever on earth is wrong with the elevator?" she said to the concierge. "I kept pushing the button, but it wouldn't come up."

"Oh, it doesn't come down," the concierge said. She smiled politely.

"What do you mean it doesn't come down?"

"It take up, but not down. You walk down."

"Why, for heaven's sake?"

The girl shrugged.

"Well, I never heard of anything so ridiculous in my life." Mrs Foster pointed to the elevator. "There it is. How on earth could it have gotten there? It had to come down."

The concierge's eyes glazed over. "Up," she said, "but you walk down."

Mrs Foster looked at me.

"We'd better go," I said tactfully.

She twitched her shoulders as if she could twitch off the city of Paris and we went outside to hail a taxi. "There are lots of good things about France," I said. "Art, wine, the people. . ."

She nodded curtly. Her lips were pressed tight together.

The Hôtel des Écoles was about the same size as the pension in the rue Cassette. There was no one behind the small counter, but through the glass office door we could see a large woman in a black dress, poring over a ledger. She raised her eyes and saw us, but made no attempt to rise. Mrs Foster looked at her and put her hands on her narrow hips. Her look said, Well. Are you going to come out and ask what we want or aren't you?

I moved to the door and called "Si'il vous plait, mam'selle."

She got up with some difficulty and opened the door. "Oui, M'sieu?"

"I want to see Missus Bell," Mrs Foster said. She clamped her lips together so that two long wrinkles appeared in each cheek. "Bell. B-E-L-L. Does she live here?"

"Bail?"

"No, Bell. I spelled it for you."

"No speak Anglais."

"Oh, for heaven's sake," Mrs Foster said.

"She is looking for her daughter," I said in French. "Her name is Hope Bell. We have been told she is living here."

The concierge shook her head. "Non, madame," she said.

Mrs Foster's hat was beginning to slip again. "Well, has she ever lived here?"

I translated.

"Non, madame," the woman said.

"Can't you say anything but no, madame, yes, madame?" Mrs Foster asked.

"Non, madame."

Mrs Foster threw up her hands. "I don't think she knows what I'm talking about," she said. Then to the concierge, "I say I don't think you know what I'm talking about."

"Non, madame."

"I'm talking about my daughter. Her name is Bell." She looked at me. "I've said it a thousand times."

"She no here."

"Well, do you know where I can find her? Where's she gone?"

"Elle sortie," the woman said to me.

"Apparently your daughter lives here," I said, "but she's out."

Mrs Foster expressed some relief. She clutched her handbag and sagged a little on her feet. I told the concierge that I lived across the street and asked her to notify me when Mademoiselle Bell returned. "She'll let me know when she comes in," I said to Mrs Foster, "and I'll bring her to you."

Exhausted, she nodded. I sent her back to her pension in a taxi.

I felt sorry for her, and I thought it might help her if I wrote a piece for the paper about her problem. The day it appeared I was in the Deux Magots and I ran into Wambly Bald. He was a short, round man who wrote a gossip column about Montparnasse called "La Vue Bohème". He said that he had read my piece. "And by the way," he said, "I think your Hope Bell is the gal who's gone off with Henry Miller. You know him?"

I didn't.

"I think they've gone off to Rambouillet. I gather she's got some dough. Maybe she's going to be his Guggenheim. He's trying to write the great American novel, and he's pretty hard up."

"If you can find out where they are, I wish you'd let me know," I said. "Her mother's really upset."

I dropped by the rue Cassette to tell Mrs Foster that I had some news. I wanted to cheer her up.

"She should be all right," I said. "She's with a writer."

"Oh, my God!" she exclaimed.

About a week later I got a pneumatique from Wambley saying that his friend Henry and Hope Bell had returned to Paris and that she was back at the Hôtel des Écoles.

By a coincidence Henry Miller was in the *Herald* offices when I got back there that day; he had come to see Elliot Paul. Elliot, always kind to literary waifs, was commissioning Henry to write a piece for the *Herald* about the Cirque Medrano. The piece did eventually appear; I think it was the first one by Henry Miller to appear in Paris.

The three of us went out to lunch. Elliot paid for Henry's meal and I paid for his Pernod.

"I understand you know Hope Bell," I said.

He sipped his milky green drink and gave me an odd look. "You know her?"

"I know about her," I said. "I haven't met her."

He shook his balding head. "She's too much for me," he said.

"Her mother's here. She wants to take her back to Minneapolis."

"I'm pretty hungry, but I couldn't go it," Henry said. "I'm afraid the only way her mother's going to get her to go is to have her arrested."

"What for?" Elliot asked.

"Oh, I don't know. Nymphomania."

Elliot laughed. "The French police will never arrest anyone for that. They won't even arrest for rape."

"She also drinks too much," Henry said.

Henry Miller was thirty-nine, fourteen years older than I. I thought that at his age he should have achieved something in his life. But there he was, a penniless emigré, an unpublished writer who knew only a smattering of French. He wore spectacles and was going bald; I did not think he was physically attractive. However, after I got to know him better, I grew to like him. He was determined to become a writer; nothing else interested him. He told me that he had written two novels which had been rejected many times. It seemed to me that at his age he had little chance of getting anywhere in the literary world.

One day he brought me a thick manuscript of more than six hundred pages, and asked me to read it. It was called *Crazy Cock*. From the start I disliked the style. It was exceedingly rough and I found its obscenity shocking. Although here and there I came upon what I thought were rich segments, the work seemed to me to be self-indulgent. I gave it back to Henry and told him that I thought the book had real possibilities but it needed cutting and polishing. It was repetitious.

Later he told me that he had cut it, by half. It was never published, but parts of it appeared in *Tropic of Cancer*, which was published in Paris in 1934. I was amazed to discover that *Tropic* caused something of a sensation. Laurence Durrell compared it to *Moby Dick* and it was called an American classic by T.S. Eliot, Ezra Pound, George Orwell and Edmund Wilson.

Writing about Henry Miller, I am reminded of Clark Gable: I knew him too before he became famous and my evaluation of his prospects were equally wide of the mark. As a youth I was a stunt man in Hollywood. I doubled for John Barrymore, Tom Mix and Leatrice Joy, among others. At that time Clark was a dress-extra: he owned a tuxedo and tails and when he wore them he was paid more than the $7.50 a day that extras earned. I lived near him, and we became friendly.

There was no Central Casting Bureau in those days of the silent film; we had to find our own jobs. Clark and I went together to call on casting offices of various studios, in my old Stutz—which had belonged to Jack Pickford—or in Clark's Dodge. We talked a lot about acting and stunt work and about the movie business in general. Clark was serious about acting, which I thought a pretty silly pursuit. I told him that if he expected to get anywhere in pictures he would have to change his name. I was only half-kidding. "Nobody with the name Clark is going to make it," I said. "Imagine that on a marquee! Terrible. And besides, your ears stick out. You should have them moved closer to your head."

"Yeh," he said, "and if you want to live to be a writer you'd better quit risking your goddam neck."

When I got home from work after meeting Henry Miller, it was too late for me to call on Hope Bell. But the next morning I crossed the street to her hotel, and the concierge confirmed that she was in her room, on the third floor. I went up and knocked. There was no answer, and I knocked several times more before an irritated contralto called, "Who is it?"

I gave her my name. "I have a message from your mother," I said. I heard some shuffling around and presently Hope answered the door. She was wearing a peignoir which hung open loosely over her transparent nightgown. Her face was puffy from sleep, but rather pretty. She swept her disheveled hair back with her hand, smiled at me, and asked me to come in. When I did, she closed the door after me and remained facing me, with her back against it.

"Your mother is here," I said, "in Paris. And she really wants to see you."

"Excuse me," she said, and went into the bathroom. I heard the tap running. When she reappeared after some time, her hair was combed and she was wearing lipstick and powder. "Where's Mother staying?"

"She's at the pension on the rue Cassette where you used to stay. We went there because she thought you were still there. She said you didn't answer her letters."

She took a cigarette from a pack on the dressing table and lighted it. "I'll get dressed," she said, and took off her peignoir. I turned my back and looked out the window.

She was a voluptuous woman, but beginning to run to fat. The sky was overcast and the tops of the buildings ran westward in waves; smoke was coming out of innumerable identical smokestacks.

"I don't know that I'm going to see her," Hope said, behind me. "We don't get along. She doesn't approve of me."

"She didn't give me that impression," I said, "She really is eager to see you. She wants to take you home."

"I'm not going. What time is it?"

"It's ten forty-five. Look," I said, turning to face her, "Your mother knows you're in town, she knows you're here. If you don't go to her, she'll come here to see you."

She was wearing a gray flannel suit. Her blouse was white, with a red scarf at the neck. "Will you go with me?"

"Well, I can't now," I said. "I have to go to work."

"Don't you have time for a drink?"

"Coffee," I said.

"I need a pick-me-up." She put on a black cloche.

We went down the stairs and out onto the street. I showed her where I lived. Then I walked her to the Dôme, but she wanted to go to the Viking, a bar about a block farther away, so we went there. There were two customers in the place when we entered; a young man asleep at a table and at the bar an older, bearded man who said hello to us in an odd accent. He had colorless hair and a mottled face; there was a big wart by the side of his large nose. A waiter was polishing glasses behind the bar. We climbed onto barstools and Hope asked the waiter, "Où est Billie?"

"Il n'a pas encore arrivé. Voulez vous prenez quelque chose?"

"I come here because of Billie," Hope said to me. "He's the patron; he's nice to me. Café fin," she said to the waiter.

I ordered coffee. She lit a cigarette and, looking at herself in the mirror behind the bar, straightened an errant lock of hair. "I don't want to see mother because she'll try to send me back to a sanitorium. I escaped from the last one." She poured the brandy into her cup. "It was a hell of a place. Full of mental misfits and derelicts, the craziest people. I hated it. It was in Colorado. They wouldn't give me anything to drink except milk. I hate milk. I'm never going to a place like that again, I don't care what happens."

At this point Billie came in. He was a chubby Englishman; everything about him was round: his eyes, his ears, his mouth and his rosy chin.

"Well, for God's sake," Hope said. "Where have you been?"

"Morning, Miss." He went behind the bar and took off his dark jacket and put on a white one. "Been doing a little shadow boxing." He danced on his toes, and threw a left and a right punch. "Getting some exercise. Haven't seen you for some time. Where you been?"

"Rambouillet."

Billie's face became suddenly serious. He leaned toward her over the bar. "Have you had anything to eat, Miss?"

"No. Don't want anything."

"You should eat something, Miss."

"I'm getting too fat. Give me another brandy."

I stood up. "I've got to go," I said. "I really urge you to go and see your mother.

"I'm thinking about it," she said, frowning. Suddenly her face creased into a bright smile. "You know where I live. Come and see me."

I did not want to become involved with her. She obviously had a lot of problems.

But several mornings later there was a knock at my

door about nine o'clock. I had been out until the wee hours, and I was still in bed. I opened the door, and Hope rushed in and threw her arms around me. She must have paid the concierge to let her come up. She kissed me; her breath smelled of alcohol.

"I'd like to go to bed with you," she said. "Would you mind?"

"That's the best offer I've had today," I said, "but I'm not awake yet."

She began to undress.

"Have you seen your mother?" I asked, making conversation.

"Not yet."

"Oh for God's sake! Look, before we go to bed, promise me you'll go and see her."

"I promise." She was now wearing only a garter belt. "I want to keep this on," she said. "Because I have a scar. From a Caesarean operation, when my child was born. Oh hell." She unhooked the belt. "You might as well see it. Isn't it nasty? Isn't it horrid? My husband said it looked like I was struck by lightning. He's got my child, you know. A nice little boy. He looks just like his dad."

She got into bed. We went through the usual sexual routine a couple of times. She wanted to go on, but I told her I had to go to work, which was true. I got up and dressed hastily.

"Don't forget your mother," I said, from the door.

I left her in my bed, and I wondered whether she would be gone when I came home that night.

IV
Pete Emerald
and the Sphynx

I received a report from New York anent Jack (Legs) Diamond:

Thirty-three years old, married, lives in Acra, Green County, New York. Born in Brooklyn where he was arrested for burglary when he was sixteen. Served a brief time in the workhouse, one of the two times he has been jailed. The other was after joining the Army in 1917: he deserted and spent six months in the Federal prison at Fort Leavenworth, Kansas. He became body-guard of Jake Orgen (Little Augie), east side gang leader, and was with him when Little Augie was killed. Diamond was also shot. He and Frankie Marlow were indicted for the murder. Police were able to arrest Marlow, but they couldn't find Diamond. Eventually he showed up with a lawyer at Police Headquarters, saying, "I understand you want to see me." He was locked up in the Tombs on the Little Augie charge. Both he and Marlow were exonerated. No witnesses.

Later drug smuggling charges were brought

against him and again he was jailed. Arnold Rothstein, for whom Diamond and his brother Eddie
worked, put up $15,000 bail-bond for Legs and Dia-
mond jumped it. The bond was forfeited. When
Rothstein was shot and killed both Legs and his
brother were arrested for the murder but released
because the prosecution was unable to produce any
witnesses.

Shortly after that, in March 1930, Legs was indicted for the murder of W. Cassidy and S. Walker in
the Hotsy Totsy Night Club, of which Legs was part
owner. Bail was denied him. He remained in jail for
ten days. He was released because the State's case col-
lapsed. No witnesses.

Jack Diamond was arrested for the twenty-third
time this year charged with the murder of G.F. Miller
in Newark. Again the prosecution let him go for lack
of evidence. It was shortly after that that he sailed for
Europe on the S.S. Belgenland.

I took the report to Eric Hawkins. After reading it, he
said, "Whew! Do you still think that's the fellow?"

I nodded.

"Well, you want to give it a try? Okay. Go ahead. But
be careful."

I went to the Hotel Continental and waited in the lobby for about an hour, but Pete didn't show up. I left a note
for him and went to Harry's New York Bar, thinking he
might be there. He wasn't. But on the way back to the
Herald, I ran into him on the rue Royale.

"Glad to see you," he said. "I've been looking for the
American Legion Post."

"It's on the rue Pierre Charron."

"Thought I'd like to go see what the joint's like. Want
to come along?"

The American Legion Post in Paris was housed in Pershing Hall, a new building which had been paid for by subscription. Veterans of the war, most of them tourists, liked to congregate there and talk over old times in the services. Pete and I went into the barroom, where a number of men were sitting around tables. The bartender, a middle-aged man with a bulbous nose and a wrinkled forehead, asked us if we belonged to the Legion.

"I was with the Hundred and Forty-seventh Field Artillery," Pete said.

I showed my press card. He wasn't impressed with it, but he held out his hand to Pete. "Welcome to the joint," he said. "What'll you have?"

Pete said he wanted a hot rum. "It's cold outside," he said, blowing on his hands. I really didn't want anything to drink, because it was the middle of the afternoon, and I had to go back to the office, but I thought I would be more comfortable talking to him if I had a little something under my belt, so I ordered a rum.

We took our drinks to a table in the corner. One of the men at a table near us got up and came over. He was a big-bellied, curly-haired top-sergeant type with a loud voice.

"I'm the commandant here," he said to Pete. "I heard you say you was with the field artillery. Handlin' the big babies, huh? You know Shorty Langhorn? I think he was in the Forty-seventh."

"I don't believe I do," Pete said. "I was in the Hundred and Forty-seventh."

"You just get here?"

"Couple days ago."

"How're things in the States?"

"Not too bad."

"Well, you've come to the right place. No Prohibition here. Just wine, women, song—anything you want you

Legs Diamond and the author at the American Legion

can have, if you got the jack. How'd you like a girl that's half Balinese, a quarter Spanish and a quarter Indian? I could fix you up with a Serbian queen, or a Russian princess. How about a pet goat from Switzerland?" He went off into a fit of loud laughter.

Someone from his table called, "Don't forget the Siamese twins."

"If you need any help, lemme know," the Commandant said. He went back to his table.

Pete asked me about Parisian brothels and I told him about a new one called The Sphynx which had opened recently near my place. He said he would like to see it. We had a second drink and I got up my courage and said, "May I ask you a personal question?"

He was on the defensive at once. "What do you wanna know?"

"There's a rumor going around that you're Jack Diamond."

He put his cup down so fast that some of his drink sloshed over the rim. "For Christ's sake! Where'd you get that idea?"

"Well, New York says that Diamond is over here. Diamond—Emerald. You know. They sort of go together."

For a few seconds he stared into my eyes. Then he leaned toward me and said, in a low voice, "Okay, okay. I'm going to square with you. My name's John Diamond. But I don't want no publicity. Don't for God's sake put anything in the paper about me."

"I won't, I promise. Not without your permission."

"You're not going to get it."

"All right then. I won't expose you. But tell me, why are you here?"

"God damn it!" he said quietly. He sat back in his chair. "I came to Europe because every piss-ant in New York was trying to rub me out. Just a couple of nights before I

left I was on my way home, and some goons drove up—
they riddled my car with bullets. It's a miracle I'm alive."
He got up, obviously disturbed. "Let's get the hell out of
here."

Outside on the street, I told him again that I would not
divulge his identity.

"Thanks kid," he said. "Say, listen, I need somebody I
can trust who speaks the language to show me around.
How about you? I'll pay for everything."

It was an offer I certainly couldn't refuse. He was a
good story and I wanted to keep track of him. "It'll have to
be after work," I said.

"I been wanting to see the Folies Bergère. How about
we go tonight? And then we can look at the new whore-
house you mentioned."

I joined Pete that night at the Continental and we took
a taxi to the Folies Théâtre. Rain was coming down heavily; through the car's lights it looked like confetti made of
gunmetal.

"Day for ducks," Pete said. "Don't it ever stop rainin'?"

I told him that once it had rained in Paris every day
for nine months. He whistled. I said some people loved
it—farmers, people who made umbrellas and overshoes,
clothes pressers and shoe shiners.

The façade of the theatre glittered with red, blue,
orange and green lights. Motorcars were driving up in
front and disgorging men in top hats and women in furs.
They all ducked and ran for the doorway; the women's
studded heels flashed in the lights. There was some con-
gestion at the entrance, where everybody was struggling
to get inside. I almost ran into a large woman who had
dropped her bag and stooped suddenly to pick it up. Pete,
coming after me, did walk into her. "Pardon, Madame," I
said, for Pete.

She smiled. "Rien alors," she said, and hurried into the foyer.

"I think that is the Duchess of Queensbury," I said to Pete.

He gave me a look. "My left tit," he said.

"You just bumped into her hunting seat."

He smiled a rare smile, and held out a fistful of francs which I took to the ticket window. When I came back I told him that all I was able to get were promenoirs; we had to stand. We entered the pit while the curtain was going up on a chorus of nearly naked dancers. "It's better standing anyway," I said. "We can get to the bar quicker."

We drifted to the right, looking for places to stand, and passing several heavily made-up women in garish dresses who smiled broadly at us. Along the way were stationed giant black attendants in red velvet long-tailed coats and knee breeches. We took our places just as Josephine Baker appeared. She was absolutely stunning, the color of milk-chocolate, and superbly graceful, agile as a deer. Her costume consisted of a bright green ostrich plume and matching shoes.

While we were at the bar during the entre-acte, a lady of the evening approached Pete. "After the show you like to come wiz me?"

"No, thanks," Pete said.

She put her arm through his. "I show you good time."

"I said no, lady." He jerked his arm away. "Screw."

"Screw? What is this?"

"Scram. Beat it."

With a gesture of indifference, she turned away. Pete said, "I'd have taken her up on it if she'd been Josephine Baker."

After the performance we rode across town to The Sphynx. It was the first brothel to be allowed in the Latin

Quarter, opening in 1929 in a large building on the avenue Edgar Quinet. There were seven floors of lavishly furnished rooms, including a movie salon, a small theatre for sexual performances, two bars and a huge reception hall. The motif was Egyptian. In Arabic on the façade was a motto which read, in translation: To Closer Cooperation in Everyday Life Between the Sexes.

A uniformed guard stood on either side of the doorway. A girl wearing a transparent blouse and a maid's apron and cap took our hats and coats. We entered a large hall, where a four-piece orchestra was playing "Love for Sale". Behind the band lights produced a waterfall effect; there were more lights under the glass dance floor. Women lounged in chairs against the wall; they all wore white silk pantaloons and pinafores.

A large fiftyish woman greeted us in English. "Good evening. You gentlemen like to see a show?"

"Sure," Pete said.

"What kind you like? Cinema?"

"No. How about the real thing?"

Madame looked at the watch she wore on a chain round her neck. "About an hour. I'll let you know." She excused herself to greet three men who had just entered the room.

Two of the girls got up and came over to us. They spoke in French, saying they were enchanted to meet us. Their names were Mimi and Claudette. Mimi took Pete's arm and I went with Claudette, who was very thin, across the dance floor to a table near the orchestra. Pete and I ordered whiskies, and the girls asked for cerises, a non-alcoholic cherry drink. Mimi kept up a steady fire of French. Pete suddenly told her to shut up. "I've always wanted to go to bed with two women," he said to me, "like Lucky Adolph. Ask 'em how much it would cost."

Claudette said a thousand francs. "The hell with that," Pete said.

The band began to play "Parlez-moi d'amour" and the girls suggested we dance. I didn't want to, but Pete and Mimi got up and sashayed about the floor. We were on our second round of drinks when Madame came up and shooed the girls away. We followed her upstairs, and Pete paid her five hundred francs for each of us—twenty dollars apiece.

"You could have had both those girls for that," I said. But he said this would be more fun.

We entered a small theatre; several men and two fully-dressed women were already seated in the audience. I was surprised to see the women. We sat on the aisle. Presently the curtain rose on a stage where three women and three men were playing strip poker. They were in high spirits and as each garment was removed there was a good deal of merriment. It was very funny until they were complete-ly naked. Then the laughter died away when they formed a daisy chain on the floor and began to indulge in oral sex. I was flabbergasted. I wanted to leave, and I nudged Pete, but he was so absorbed he did not notice. I felt degraded and ashamed. For the finale they all rose, and the men lifted the women to their hips and they fornicated as they left the stage.

Presently a woman came out wearing only a scarf and carrying a small dog. This was too much for me. "I'll see you downstairs," I whispered to Pete, and fled.

I waited for him at the bar for quite a while. When he finally appeared I asked him if he'd gotten his money's worth. "Hell, yes," he said. "Damndest thing I ever saw. You should have stayed."

We walked outside, bade each other good-night, and Pete climbed into a taxi. I went home on foot.

I've finally finished my novel [I wrote Mother] and it's on its way to an agent in New York. It's entitled *Gun Girl* and it's about a young woman who had a meteoric career robbing cigar stores in New York City. You may remember reading about her. I covered the story for the *American*. She plundered the stores to finance a heroin habit. Her hairbreadth escapes were front-page news; the papers called her 'the bob-haired bandit'. I followed her trail to the Women's Prison on Welfare Island, where I interviewed her. She turned out to be rather simple-minded; she had been turned onto drugs and a criminal career by a junkie she had fallen in love with. It wasn't a new story, but it had an element of tragedy. Anyway, I'm glad it's finished at last.

I've been seeing a lot of Ludwig Lewisohn. You remember you sent me a copy of his *Stephen Escott*, which I read. It's well-written but the story is weak. We've sat and talked several times in the Dôme Café, and I've enjoyed it. He is concerned about racial prejudice, which is understandable, since he's a Jew. He uses his writing as a method of battling for Jewish equality, also understandable. I learned a great deal about Jewish psychology and the Jewish attitude toward other groups from his *The Island Within*. I agree with him that Jews should be proud of their heritage. I think actually everyone should be proud of his heritage. On the other hand I don't like chauvinism—great pride in ancestors and birth places. That is an outstanding British fault. I think that a man should respect his heritage, which he really had no hand in, but he should be proud only of what he himself has done in life.

The weather is still cold and rainy. This morning I nearly froze while I was waiting for the bathtub, down the hall, to fill with warm water. But spring is on the way, thank God. I hope you are well and enjoying prolonged happiness.

V

A Death, a Meeting and
a Visit to a Hospital

It occurred to me to ask the American Consulate to help me persuade Hope Bell to go home. The Vice-Chancellor, Robert Murphy, was a friend of mine. He was a tall, blond, charming man who was to become famous as an emissary of the State Department during the second World War. I told him about Hope and her mother and asked him if there was any legal way to solve the problem.

"I don't know of any law," he said. "But maybe I could be persuasive in my official position. Why don't you bring her in?"

"That won't be easy," I said. "She won't come if she suspects we're trying to get rid of her. But if I can get her to come, you may be able to do the trick. She's very susceptible to handsome men." He laughed.

The next morning before work I went across the street to the Écoles. The concierge said that Mademoiselle was in her room. I felt I might need some defense, so I gave the concierge ten francs and asked her to go up with me. She led the way upstairs: she was wearing brown cotton stockings with clocks; the heels had been darned with multicolored threads which flashed black, white, gray and brown out of her lopsided, wide shoes at every step she took. We reached the fifth floor, and she stopped to catch her breath. Then she knocked on the door. No answer. She knocked again. No answer. She looked at me. She had not seen Mademoiselle leave since she came in yesterday; she must be in there. I suggested she use the master key.

"Attendez," she said. The key would not fit in the lock. "Alors." She stooped to look through the keyhole. "Elle est là," she said, straightening up. "Regardez." I bent to look. The key was in the lock. I pounded and called her name. Still no answer. How could we get in? There was no other door to the room, and the window was impossible. We would have to force the door.

The concierge was horrified. "Mais non, Monsieur! Mais non!"

But it was very important, I said. Mademoiselle might be ill, she might be unconscious. She might be dead.

Then call the police, she said.

I beat heavily on the door. "Hope!" I cried. "Are you there? Please answer me!" An adjoining door opened; a red-haired woman stuck her head out, and looked at us irritably.

I asked her if she had seen Hope.

"Non!" she said. "Mein Gott!" and slammed her door.

I told the concierge I was going to fetch a policeman, and ran down the stairs two at a time.

There was a policeman standing in front of the Rotonde. As calmly as I could, I explained the circumstances. He listened with exasperating indifference, picking his teeth, and then nodded and began to amble toward the pension. In the lobby he asked me how many flights we would have to climb. When I told him, he said, "Merde!"

He remained nonchalant when we reached Hope's door. He asked me who I was, although I had already told him. I presented my press card, which he examined thoughtfully. Then he asked me why I was so eager to break into the room; had it occurred to me that the tenant might not want her door opened? She might have reasons of her own for not answering the door. Perhaps she was not alone. I could see there was only one way he could be brought to cooperate with me, and reluctantly pressed two ten-franc notes into his hand. At once he was transformed. He stepped back and told me to go ahead.

I threw my weight against the door. It did not give. But the second time it did give way and I lurched into the room. Hope lay across the bed, wearing only her pink garterbelt. She looked as though she had fallen backward. Her peignoir lay on the floor; I snatched it up and threw it over her. The gendarme entered casually, his cape-jacket swinging on his shoulders. He still had the toothpick in his mouth. I put my hand on Hope's chest, and then held her wrist. She felt cold: there was no pulse. Her eyes were open slightly. I looked at the concierge, who stood in the doorway, wide-eyed, with her hand to her mouth.

"Elle est morte," I said.

I went immediately to see Mrs Foster. She was sitting in a red plush rocking chair near the window reading a book. She seemed surprised to see me. "Oh," she said, "It's you, young man." She closed the book and took off her pince-nez.

Why do I have to do this? I thought. "I hope I'm not intruding," I said.

"Oh, not at all. Won't you sit down?"

I sat on the edge of a straight chair, indicating that I did not intend to stay long. "I'm just on my way to work."

"I just had the worst excuse for a Thanksgiving dinner you could find in the world," she said. "I always thought French cooking was supposed to be so good. Can you imagine—veal for Thanksgiving?" She paused, and looked at me. "I suppose you're here because you've seen Hope."

"Yes, ma'am."

"When is she coming to see me?"

I could not meet her eyes. "I'm afraid she's not coming."

"Not coming? Not coming to see her mother?"

"I'm very sorry, Mrs Foster," I said. I took a deep breath. "But . . . well . . . your daughter is dead."

She leaned forward. Her eyes looked very big. "What's that? What's that you say?"

"The police found her in her room," I said miserably. "She seems to have had a heart attack. It was very sudden. She didn't have any pain."

Her mouth fell open. "Hope's dead," she said.

"Yes, it was very sudden. She didn't feel anything."

She took a lacey handkerchief from her sleeve and pressed it against her mouth with a veined, boney hand. Her eyes were filled with tears; she turned her head to look out the window. After a few moments she dabbed her eyes with the handkerchief. She made no sound. It was a painful scene.

"I can't tell you how sorry I am, Mrs Foster. I'll do everything I can to help you."

"Thank you, you're very kind."

"There will be police formalities."

"I'm glad her father did not live to see this."

I got up. "You'll want to take the—her—back to Minneapolis, won't you?"

"What? Oh. I don't know. I'll have to think."

I sat down again on the edge of the chair. "There has to be an autopsy, but then I'll put an undertaker in charge. Whatever you want done will be done."

She dabbed at her eyes again. "I knew she shouldn't have come here. She never had anything wrong with her heart. I had a feeling that if she came here I'd never see her again."

"Please remember that it all happened quickly. That should be a comfort. There couldn't have been any pain. It was quick."

"I just knew she shouldn't have come. I told her not to come."

We sat for an agonizingly long time without speaking. I tried desperately to think of something else to say, but I couldn't. She looked out the window. Finally I stood up. "I'm sorry. I have to go now."

She picked up the book and clasped it in both hands. It was *Science and Health.* She seemed to cling to it as though it were a sort of raft in a stormy sea. "I'll take her home," she said sadly, "and bury her beside her father."

I wrote to Mother about Hope Bell.

There were so many things I could not include in my news story about her and her mother that it was little more than perfunctory. It just about boiled down to the headline, "Art Student Dies of Heart Attack".

That's one of the sad things about newspaper writing. It so often just scratches the surface.

I've been promoted. I am now assigned to the Embassy-Consulate beat, which means that I call on them every day to gather news. Confreres say that this is the most important job on the paper; if this is true it makes me the star reporter. Next week I am going to Nancy with Ambassador Edge, erstwhile Governor of New Jersey. He's going to receive an honorary degree from the university there—I don't much care for that custom. It seems to me it's just a method of promoting an institution by catering to the egos of the recipients. But I won't say so in the story I write—mainly because some day I'd like that honor myself.

Have I mentioned George Rehm, the *Herald's* sports editor? His wife Mary is going to have a baby and so is Waldo Pierce's mistress, Alzira. Waldo and Alzira have just come here from Maine; Waldo's family owns some forest land there. They expect to get married soon, maybe just after the baby is born. Waldo is an important artist, a great big man with a beard. He is sort of famous for having set out on a cattle boat from Boston to Europe with John Reed, the "Soviet Saint", whom he knew from Harvard, and about sixteen miles out decided he couldn't stand the smelly accommodations and dove overboard and swam back to Boston. Hell of a guy. I was in Lipps the other night, where the German beer is the best in Paris, with him and Alzira and the Rehms. Eve Le Gallienne was there, wearing a sailor cap and a painted moustache. She lives here with her father. Glenway Westcott sat with us for a while. I haven't read his recent book, *The Baby's Bed,* but I have read his *The Grandmothers* and I thought it was very good.

While I'm trying to keep you amused by and informed of my current activities and the celebrities I associate with, don't let me forget Brand Whitlock, the former Ambassador to Belgium. I interviewed him the other day. He has written a biography of Lafayette. It seems to me that everybody on God's earth is writing or has written a book. Whitlock is a tall, gentle man. He was very nice, and after he told me about himself and the book, *he* interviewed *me!* That was quite a switch. I told him about my novel, and he suggested I send the manuscript to his publisher. I'm going to suggest it to Jean Wick, my agent.

Did I write you that I saw Pepe Lederer, Marion Davies' niece? I knew her in California. She's on a European tour and came to see me at the paper, so I invited her out to dinner. She went with me, breaking an engagement with Anita Loos and John Emerson (there I go, name dropping again). We had a pleasant evening, hashing over Hollywood. I told her I thought she should get out of the unreal atmosphere she was living in, with Marion Davies and William Randolph Hearst. I think I persuaded her to go to the University of Geneva and study French.

I was wrong about Pepe Lederer. She did go to school in Switzerland, but after one term she went to California and committed suicide by jumping from a hospital window.

I learned through the Embassy that Charles Gates Dawes was coming to Paris. He was a Chicago banker who had served as Vice President under Calvin Coolidge and was at that time U.S. Ambassador to the Court of Saint James. I met him at the Gare St. Lazare; he had just come in from London.

At that time the public image of a banker was a humorless, conservative fellow who smoked a big cigar and smiled thinly when you made a deposit and looked mean when you wanted a loan. Dawes was certainly not like that. He was gracious, charming and debonair. When I began to interview him he interrupted and apologized, saying he was late for an appointment with Jo Davidson, who had been commissioned by the U.S. Government to sculpt a bust of him for the Senate Gallery. "Why don't

The author interviewing Charles Dawes who poses for Jo Davidson

you come along later on to Davidson's studio?" he said. "We can have a chat there." I was delighted.

A maid ushered me into the studio, where the Ambassador was sitting in a straight-backed chair on a platform. Davidson, a muscular, dynamic man, was hacking away at a block of marble. When I came in Dawes was talking about a visit he had recently made to an archeological dig in southern France where evidence had been discovered of pre-Ice Age people. He interrupted himself to introduce me to Davidson, and to Lincoln Steffens, the muckraker and humorist, who was also in the room.

Then he continued his story, saying that he had concluded from the evidence he had seen that today's homo sapiens should not consider themselves important. "That goes for pontiffs, princes and politicians," he said, and chuckled. "We are all mere plankton on the waves of time."

I asked him for permission to quote that remark.

"Oh, no," he said, with a wry smile. "I'm afraid it would offend some of my colleagues in Washington. But it's true: mankind would be better off and life would be a lot more enjoyable if people—especially so-called big shots and muckety-mucks—took themselves less seriously."

I said I thought this comment from a person of his stature might carry some weight. Steffens agreed with me; he didn't see why it shouldn't be quoted.

Dawes went on posing for a couple of hours and then invited all of us to lunch with him at the Ritz. Midway through his second martini he consented to let me quote him. I hurried back to the office and wrote the story. It carried my by-line and was picked up by the wire services and reprinted around the world.

That wasn't the only fortuitous thing that happened

to me because of my acquaintance with Charles Gates
Dawes. It was through him that I met Patricia Warington.
While he was in Paris Dawes gave a cocktail party at his
suite at the Ritz. I was invited. I saw an incredible beauty
there: a short, retroussé nose, full lips, wavy chestnut
hair. . . It was Patricia. Her father was a Chicago banker,
an associate of Dawes. She had come to Paris with her
mother to study music and steep herself in culture. I set
out at once to charm her. I wanted to marry her, or
anyway get close to her somehow.

I tried of course to impress her, by telling her that I
was not just a newspaperman; I was a writer, who had in
fact just written a book. I told her how I had caught
writing fever with my doggerel in the *Birmingham Age-
Herald* when I was seven years old. She seemed suitably
impressed.

"How about you?" I asked. "You play the piano."

"Yes, but I don't expect to set the world on fire doing
it. How did you get to be a reporter?"

I told her that after my freshman year at college my
mother sent me a hundred dollars and told me I was on
my own. I drifted—became a bellboy on an ocean liner
and eventually wound up in Hollywood as a movie stunt
man. I was offered a job as an actor but I turned it down
to become a newspaperman.

"That's the story of my life," I said. "Now tell me
yours."

"Oh, I'm afraid mine hasn't been that exciting. In fact,
it's dull. I was born and brought up in Chicago, went to
Miss Porter's School and Vassar and made my debut
about two years ago; the highlight of that was that I was
received by Queen Mary. Really, the only interesting thing
about me now is that I'm about to be married."

"Married!" I said, without thinking. "To whom? When?"

"Soon. To Count Charles de Rouselle."

"Well, I'm not surprised," I said, although I was. "You're too beautiful to be running around loose."

I felt as though I had been punched in the stomach. But when I learned that her fiancé was in the south of France for a prolonged stay, I invited her to join me for a bridge game with Elliot Paul and his new wife. She accepted.

The bridge party took place the night before I was to leave for Nancy with Ambassador Edge. It was a great success: we laughed and drank a lot of wine. It was after midnight when I took her home. We were both pretty tight, which may be why she permitted me to kiss her goodnight. It was quite a kiss. When I finally got to bed I couldn't sleep: I kept thinking about that kiss, and I was tense because I had to get up early to catch the train. The Gare de l'Est was a long way from my place. Sure enough, when I finally fell asleep I overslept and I didn't have time even to have a cup of coffee, which would have helped my raging hangover. I went to the station by subway, lugging a suitcase which contained my tuxedo for the ceremonial ball, a typewriter and my overcoat. I got to the station about two minutes to nine. Luckily I had my ticket from the Embassy so I was able to run through the waiting room to the gate. The train was already moving; I shoved my typewriter and case onto the platform of the last car, gripped a handrail and swung myself aboard.

I was completely out of breath. After I recovered a bit, I picked up my possessions and walked down the corridor to a compartment with only two occupants: an emaciated woman and a man with a straggly beard. I stashed my luggage on the rack, folded my overcoat over it, bade the two passengers "Bon jour" and worked my way through the cars looking for the Ambassador's private car. I finally found it, several cars beyond the diner. The press attaché, Robert Pell, exclaimed, "Ah ha! There you are! We were wondering what happened to you." The Ambassador and his retinue were wearing striped trousers and frock coats. Even the *Tribune* reporter, Kosputh, was tastefully attired in a dark blue suit and tie. I was very much out of place in my brown tweeds and red necktie. And all the seats were taken: I had to perch on the arm of Kosputh's chair.

Ambassador Edge got up and shook my hand. "So you almost missed the train," he said. "That would have been a calamity."

"My alarm didn't go off," I said lamely.

He said he was glad I made it, and I thanked him. It was beginning to rain; big drops spattered the windows, blurring the scene. The red-roofed houses in the villages looked fresh and clean, but the cattle standing in the fields appeared woebegone. At noon we all went into the diner for lunch. Pell, Kosputh, the naval attaché and I sat at a table together. I had heard that Kosputh, who was an Armenian, had recently married a Turkish woman. I asked him about it. He said they had met in Constantinople; her father was a shipowner who operated a fleet in the Black Sea. The Naval attaché commented on feelings among the Armenians toward the Turks, and Kosputh said the whole thing had been like the Capulets and the Montagues. "Our friends call us Romeo and Juliet," he said.

Pell ordered the wine, a Strasbourg white. It was very good, and my hangover vanished. The food was typical French railroad: hors-d-oeuvre, pork chop, lettuce salad, cheese and fruit. During the meal the train stopped at

Bar-le-Duc, and by the time we finished we were nearing Nancy.

I got up from the table. "I'd better get my things," I said, and made my way toward the rear of the train. I reached the end of the car behind the diner and saw, to my astonishment, that it was the last car. There was nothing behind it but wet tracks. For a moment I thought I had lost my mind. I rushed back to the dining car and asked the steward, in some agitation, what had happened to the rear cars. He said they had been switched off at Bar-le-Duc. My typewriter, my most valuable possession, was gone—I might never see it again. And my other things were certainly important to me. I felt helpless and frantic, like a man who has come home to find his house on fire.

The platform at Nancy was covered with red carpet; a reception committee was lined up of dignitaries in long-tailed coats and stove-pipe hats. Behind them stood a troop of soldiers in dress regalia, including brass helmets. As the train glided to a stop a band struck up "The Star Spangled Banner."

The moment the porter opened the door to the Ambassador's car, I, in my anguish, leaped down the steps before anyone else, surprising the reception committee. I strode up and down in front of them, shouting, "Où est le chef-de-gare? Où est le chef-de-gare?" The city and university officials stared at me aghast; I think they thought the Ambassador had been assassinated. Someone quickly found the station master. I told him what had happened, and demanded to know why the train had been chopped in two without any warning. He promised to do what he could to rescue my belongings. While I was haranguing him, the Ambassador and his party were ceremoniously received by the relieved dignitaries and taken to waiting automobiles. I hurried after them.

The actual presentation of the honorary degree to the

Ambassador was not much of an event. Mr Edge was kissed on both cheeks. I tried to embellish the story, forced as I was to write in pencil, and filed it from the post office. Since I could not attend the ceremonial banquet in my tweeds, I had to eat dinner alone in a small café, feeling sorry for myself. The only saving grace for the whole thing was that news was scarce the day my story arrived at the paper, so they played it on the front page.

I returned to Paris. Days went by and I heard nothing of my lost effects. Then one morning I got a call from Pell at the Embassy; my suitcase, typewriter and overcoat had been returned, "from somewhere in Russia".

That was a cheerful note, but the rest of the week was not a pleasant one. For one thing, I got into a brawl at the annual dinner of the Anglo-American Press Club, which was held at the Lido. My antagonist was John Herman, who represented United Press in Moscow. He was in Paris on his way home to New York. I can't vouch for him, or for anyone else at the dinner, but I was feeling no pain. Herman bumped into me, apparently inadvertently, and I felt I was being pushed around: I have strong inferiority feelings. There was a boxing ring there, used for exhibition bouts during dinner, and I invited Herman to join me in the ring to redress the insult. He suggested I forget it, but I insisted and we both paid for my stubborness.

We were in the heat of battle when we both realized that we had no referee, no time keeper, and no judges, although we did have an audience of our colleagues. We staggered on until we could hardly raise our arms. He had a bloody nose, and I had a black eye. Finally I apologized, we embraced each other and went to the bar, where we toasted to our everlasting friendship. He was a perfect gentleman throughout, and I acted like a perfect idiot.

I had not recovered from that evening when I had to

go into the American Hospital for a hemorrhoid operation. I think my affliction was due to drinking too much.
If that was really the case, there must have been an
epidemic of hemorrhoids in Paris.

After the operation I was wheeled into a two-bed
room. The man in the other bed was a septuagenarian
American from Bucyrus, Ohio, who had had a kidney
operation. He was a retired preacher named Elmer Long.
He had a hooked nose, and his unshaven face was con-
cave, partly because he had taken out his false teeth. Almost as soon as I came out of the anesthesia he began to
tell me about his life. He apparently needed to confide in
someone. He said his wife had died a year or so earlier,
and he had come to Paris to see the sights. Before that he
had never been farther away from Bucyrus than Chicago.

"I never took a drink in my life before my wife died,"
he said. "and I never played around with the choir girls.
Until she left me I was as good as gold. Then one day,
after she died, I got me a bottle of bootleg whiskey and
drank it right down. I wanted to see what it was like. For
years I had preached against the demon rum and I had
never tasted the stuff. 'Course I got drunk and I had an
automobile accident. It got around town that I drank, and
people started avoiding me. I got lonely, and that's why I
left. I had given that town the best years of my life and it
turned its back on me when I needed help. So I came over
here where I can drink if I want to, and do whatever I
please."

"Then you don't want to go back to Bucyrus?"

"Well, I'd like to die there, but I don't think I'll live to
go home. I'd like to be buried next to Lucy."

His doctor was a large, florid man with bushy eyebrows, a loud cheerful voice, and a fierce toothy smile
like Teddy Roosevelt's.

"Howdy Elmer. How you doin'?"

"Oh, pretty good, Doc. There's just a little pain on this side."

"What do you mean, pain? Why, if I was as well as you I'd get the hell out of bed and run around the block. How much water'd you drink today?"

"Well, not much, Doc, because I can't drink much, Doc."

"Now I've told you to drink, and by God you'd better drink or I'm gonna bring in a blacksnake whip and we're going to tangle. You hear? I want you to drink lots of water."

"Well, okay, Doc, I'll try."

The doctor filled a glass from a pitcher and handed it to Elmer. "Here. Drink this." While Elmer obeyed, he said, "You'll never be able to get out of here and use that whang of yours if you don't drink lots of water." He laughed and slapped the old man on his sheet-covered thigh. "Maybe you don't want to use it any more. Maybe you're through with that foolishness."

"No, sir, Doc, I ain't through yet. I still got some juice. I'll drink the water if it kills me."

"That's right," the doctor said jovially. "Because if you don't, I'll have to cut a hole in your belly."

"I don't want to go through that again," Elmer said. He lay back with a sigh as the doctor bustled out.

Later on when I felt better I talked to Elmer about religion. I was curious to know why he had turned away from it. I told him I had been raised as an Episcopalian; my grandmother had started taking me to church when I was seven years old, and I had sung in the choir. But I never liked it. "The older I got the more boring I thought it was," I said.

Elmer sipped his water. "You're an agnostic," he said. "That's not good. You'll end up in purgatory."

"What was it turned you off?"

"Oh, I think I stayed with it too long. I fought the Devil, but I never knew who he was. I thought I was saving people from damnation; it came to me that I was battling windmills."

I told him that I was toying with the idea of starting a new religion—a religion of beauty and laughter.

"You mean you're going to tell jokes?" Elmer asked. He was incredulous.

"Well," I said, "it's part of life—humor. I mean, if people couldn't laugh, they would die." It occurred to me suddenly that I had not seen Elmer laugh since I had met him.

"You won't get anywhere with that religion," he said mournfully. "People like to congregate and they like to have rules and regulations. The harder you make it for 'em the better they like it."

When I left the hospital in a few days Elmer was still in bed, sadly sipping water. I thought I would probably never see him again.

VI
Pete Emerald Again

I recuperated in Neuilly, at a house owned by Priscilla and Lacy Kastner. King Carol of Roumania had stayed there during his exile. When I got back to Paris, I looked up Pete Emerald. He told me he wanted to visit a gambling club; there were several in Paris. Before the war there had been a chic gambling resort, like Deauville, at Enghein, an hour's drive away. But it had been closed by the government because of a scandal. Since then a number of baccarat clubs had been started in the city: baccarat in duly constituted clubs was legal in France. None of these clubs were strictly gambling houses; they all had literary or social façades and they were all licensed by the city fathers, who drew off the lion's share of the receipts. The French called these clubs tripots, which also means houses of ill fame.

The most notorious one was the Haussmann, on the boulevard des Italiens. It supposedly existed to encourage art and music, but of course the majority of its members were interested only in gambling. One could dine there, but there was no dance floor; baccarat tables filled most of the rooms. The place was reasonably exclusive; there was a rule that the names of proposed members had to be posted for three weeks before they could be allowed to play. But it was a rule that was often broken. In any case, my press card got us instant admittance.

The rooms were palatial, and crowded with a me-lange of nationalities: French, English, Americans, Greeks and Argentinians. There were also a number of ladies of the evening, and other ladies wearing a lot of valuable jewelry. The air was heavy with cigar smoke.

Pete wanted to play at the table with the 20,000 franc limit. He bought ten large iron chips, each of which was worth 10,000 francs or $400, and sat next to a rouged and bejeweled older woman who toyed carelessly with her pile of chips. On his left was a man with bushy eyebrows and a tuxedo stretched over his embonpoint. This man was the banker for the next drawing; he had the "shoe", the instrument in which the cards were held. He pushed a stake of 20,000 francs over the green cloth of the table to the croupier. Since Pete was on the banker's right, he had the first chance to bet, either the whole amount or any part of it. Pete hesitated. Green-shaded lamps hung low over the table, casting a sickly glow over the tense faces of the players. I was standing behind Pete. One of the pros-titutes came up and stood next to me. She was about thir-ty, well-groomed and pretty. She had obviously become interested in Pete because of his large stack of chips.

Pete put up two of his heavy chips. "I'll shoot the works," he said.

The winning number at baccarat is nine. Slowly the banker dealt four cards, two to Pete and two to himself. Pete's cards were a jack and a six. Face cards counted ten, so the jack was no good. The banker asked Pete if he wanted another card and after some deliberation he said no. He could win if his six was closer to nine than either or both of the banker's cards.

The banker turned his cards up. They were a king and a three. He took another. It was an eight. With the count of eleven—three and eight—the banker was broke. Pete raked in the chips; he became the banker and pushed two of the chips onto the playing field. The croupier asked the rouged woman on Pete's right if she would like to bet the "banco". She passed, in an American accent. So did two other players, but the fourth, a big, heavy-set man with a black-and-white beard covering his wing collar, tossed out equal chips. Pete dealt the cards, got an eight, and won again. There was some whispering around the table. Pete lit a cigarette and ordered a whisky. His face was blank. I sensed he was having a good time.

Once again he won and decided to go to the no-limit table while his luck was good. The poule followed him; the table was in another room. I went to the five-franc minimum table, where I played for about an hour, until Pete returned. He said he was ready to leave. The poule was still with him. "We'll take this lady home," he said. I asked him how he had done; he said he lost a few bucks. But the girl said, "He was verree luckee." Pete retrieved her fur coat from the hatcheck girl and we went out the swinging door to the street. I hailed a taxi. "You go on," I said. "Have a good time. I'm going home."

They went off in the cab, and Pete told me later what happened then.

She lived on the fourth floor of a modern apartment building with an elevator. The living room was furnished in expensive but quiet taste. Pete was impressed. He noticed that she closed the front door, but did not lock it. She hung her coat in a closet in the hall and then opened a double door, revealing a bedroom with a very large bed. Standing in the bedroom doorway, she said, "Here we are. You like to come in?"

Pete removed his trenchcoat and dropped it on a chair. "Sure." he said. "You sure are a good-lookin' broad."

"What is that—a broad?"

He went up to her and put his hands on her hips. "Right here's where dames're broad," he said. "You're a broad baby, that's what you are." He gave her a playful tap, and she grimaced. Then she smiled and turned to enter the bedroom. "Wait a minute," Pete said. "You and this dump look like plenty of dough. How much is this little party gonna cost me?"

She turned back to him, put her hands on either side of his face, and kissed him on the mouth. "We no talk money," she said. "My husband, he is reech man."

"Uh huh," Pete said. He was beginning to smell a mouse. "When's he coming home?"

She shrugged. "He is in Nice." She went into the bathroom.

Pete took off his jacket and vest and was unbuttoning his shirt when he heard a noise at the front door. He stood motionless, listening, and began to button his shirt again. The lady came out of the bathroom wearing a lace negligée. "What ees the matter?" she asked. "Why you no take off your costume?"

Pete walked quickly across the living room and flung open the door to the hall. A man was standing there wearing a homburg and a tuxedo under a black overcoat; he was swarthy, with a flat nose and small black eyes. He looked surprised.

"What the hell do you want?" Pete said. The man's hands were in his coat pockets; Pete thought he saw the bulge of a gun.

The stranger frowned fiercely "Qui êtes vous?" he asked.

"Get lost," Pete said. "We're busy." He began to close the door. The stranger pulled the pistol from his pocket and pointed it steadily at him. Pete stepped back, the man entered and closed the door behind him, locking it.

"What do you do here with my wife?" he asked.

"I was invited," Pete said. He moved suddenly, hitting the man's jaw with his right hand so hard that his head snapped back, and catching his gun arm with his left. A struggle ensued, a delicate table and several knick-knacks crashed to the floor with them. Pete landed on top, and struggled to get the revolver, the poule pulling ineffectually at his collar and pounding his back. He shook her off and got up with the gun in his hand. He signalled the intruder to the divan and told him to lie down on his face.

"Get me a towel," Pete said to the woman.

"No!" she said. She stamped her feet. "No, no! Go, you go!"

"Listen, baby," he said. He grasped her wrist none too gently, and she winced. "I hope I don't have to smack you too. Now you get me a towel, I'm going to tie up this lousy pimp."

She hesitated. "What you do with heem?"

"I'm gonna quiet him down so we can have our little affair in peace. Maybe he'll enjoy it. I'll leave the door open. Now bring me that towel!"

She brought it, and he used it and his belt to tie the man up. Then he resumed his evening with the woman, whose name was Renée.

I don't know if this whole story is true, but it rang true. If it was true that was one pair of con people who had got hold of the wrong pigeon.

Shortly after that memorable evening, Pete invited Sparrow Robertson and me to the races at Longchamps. Sparrow had told him that he knew more about betting on horses than anyone alive and Pete wanted him to prove it. "The only way to bet on horses," Sparrow said, "is to get to the trainers and jockeys. Otherwise, it's a losin' proposition." He said he knew all these people intimately; they were all his pals.

On one of my days off we went to the races. Before each race Sparrow conferred with his horsey friends; he was getting the dope, he said. Pete and I bet the way he did. Pete, as befit his nature, bet extravagantly, while Sparrow and I tried to hold our risks to a minimum. We won only a couple of races and lost all the others. Each time we lost, Sparrow blamed the condition of the track, the misjudgment of the trainer or the dishonesty of the jockey. Trying to make a joke out of it, I said my mother would have blamed our bad luck on the juxtaposition of the stars. "Maybe it's sun spots," I said. Sparrow looked hurt.

Between the races we dropped in at one of the race-track bars. Thanks to Sparrow's tips we were all broke, so Pete had to go back to the Continental Hotel to get some money from a stash he kept in his room; he had offered to take us to dinner. We were pretty well oiled when we went up to the desk to get his key.

"There are two gentlemen here to see you, Mr. Emerald," the concierge said.

"To see me?" Pete stiffened. "What do they want?"

"I don't know, m'sieur. They are from the Sûreté."

"What the hell is that?"

"It's the police," I said.

Two men in plain clothes who had been sitting in the

lobby got up and came over to us. They looked grim. The taller of the two showed Pete his credentials; in good English he asked to speak to him privately. "These are my pals," Pete said. "They can hear what you got to say. What do you want?"

Sparrow and I showed our press cards to the policemen. Sparrow put his arm through Pete's. "This is my old pal," he said. "What's the matter?"

Pete suggested that we go into the bar and have a drink. We all settled down at a round corner table. The three of us ordered scotch; the detectives asked for beer. The taller man drew forth an official-looking document and put it on the table in front of Pete who, of course, could not read it. "What the hell's it about?" he asked irritably.

I picked it up and read it. Then I looked at Pete. "You've got twenty-four hours to get out of France."

"Why? What have I done?"

"You are not wanted here," the tall detective said. He shrugged. "You've done something in New York. You are gangster, no? You went to England. They didn't want you, no? You went to Germany; they didn't want you, no? Let me see your passport."

"And if I don't?"

He shrugged again. "We take you to jail."

Pete dropped his passport on the table. The detective picked it up. "This is issued to John Diamond," he said. "Thirty-three years old. This is your picture. You are not Monsieur Emerald, as you called yourself. You are John Diamond."

"If that's what it says," Pete said.

"You leave tomorrow."

"For where?"

"The States."

"How about Italy?"

"They won't have you there either."

"Well, I'll be goddamned!" Pete said. He drained his glass. There was a pause. Then he looked at me and Sparrow, and said, "Well, I guess I have to go home."

The next day the police escorted him to the station and put him on a train for Cherbourg. No passenger ships were due to sail for several days so he was booked on a freighter bound for Philadelphia. I saw him off on the train. The last thing he said to me was, "I'm glad I'm going to Philly and not New York. Maybe I can get home in one piece."

Now that he was leaving, I could write a story about him, but I didn't want to. For one thing I had promised him I wouldn't, and for another I did not want to name the ship and its destination. Too many people would lie in wait for him. Since Sparrow and I were the only newsmen who knew the story, it was not written.

I kept track of Diamond through the newspapers. He got home all right. But after he returned to New York he was shot five times in the Hotel Monticello on West 64th Street. The Commissioner of Police told the press, "He was in his pyjamas when two men came to his door. There is every reason to believe that Diamond did not expect them to shoot him. He must have admitted them to his room. There is also reason to believe that the gunmen had a conversation with him, perhaps an argument, before they shot him."

The gunmen fled down the stairs. Diamond managed to find his way to the elevator. He was rushed to the hospital in an ambulance. He had been shot in the right thigh, the left abdomen, twice in the chest, and in the forehead. The forehead shot had glanced off the bone, leaving a laceration but not penetrating the skull. When he was asked how he had managed to leave his room, Pete was quoted as saying, "I took two good slugs of whisky and I made it."

He was sent to Welfare Island Hospital, where he stayed for six weeks, and made a miraculous recovery. He returned to his home at Acra, New York. Then in April, 1931, while he was having dinner with a male friend at the Saratoga Inn near Ciro, New York, he was shot in the back. His companion vanished immediately. Legs was driven fifty miles to Albany Hospital. He refused to tell the police the name of his companion, or whether he knew who had shot him. Newspapers featured the story prominently and Franklin D. Roosevelt, then Governor of New York, became very angry. He told the state police that they had to try to put an end to gang murders. "It's a sad commentary on our state," he said, "that we can't put these people in jail."

Legs was arrested in the hospital, charged with carrying a concealed weapon. Federal and state authorities vied to be the first to try him. The Feds wanted him on an old narcotics charge which had been dormant since 1927. When he was able to leave the hospital he appeared in a county court with his attorney and was exonerated from the concealed weapons charge because the prosecution was not able to prove that the pistol in question was his. The Federal charge had to be dropped because the witnesses had all disappeared.

Then, in December 1931, while he was driving his car on a road not far from his farm, Legs was shot again. This time he was killed. He was thirty-four years old.

I felt very sad when I heard of his death. He was an interesting, complicated character. He seemed cold and without any emotion, and he was certainly tough and ruthless. But he had a kind of moral side. He kept his word: if he said he would do something he could be counted on to do it. He did not commit himself often. He was generous and had tremendous courage. Somehow in his early years he had gotten on the wrong side of society, and he stayed there. If he had been on the other side he might have been remembered as a remarkable man.

He got his nickname when he was only a kid, because of his long legs and because he could easily outrun the police.

Franklin Roosevelt

VII
F.D.R. and a Wedding

Governor Franklin Delano Roosevelt of New York
came to Paris on vacation, and I was assigned to interview
him. It was a red letter day in two respects; I had been invited to have dinner with Patricia Warington and her
mother that evening at their apartment.

I went to meet Roosevelt at Gare St Lazare. As I came
up, his son James was just lifting him into a wheelchair
on the platform. The Governor greeted me graciously,
and answered my questions as I strolled along beside his
wheelchair. He said he had fled to Paris to get away from
politics.

"Then you've come to the wrong place," I said.
"There's a lot of it here."

He laughed. "I know."

"How about the rumor that you plan to run for President?"

He smiled and patted his legs. "I can't run," he said.

"That's not true," James said. "If they want him to run, he'll run."

"Pay no attention to him," Roosevelt said. "He's just my son."

"It's a good quote," I said.

"Then quote him, not me."

I wrote up the story and put it on Spencer Bull's desk. He was the new city editor—a short, stocky man with a shock of white hair. He had been a newsman in Paris for several years and his reputation was abysmal. To everyone's horror and dismay, he had been hired only the day before by Laurence Hills, the director of the *Herald*. Apparently Bull had wandered into a bar where Hills was lapping up juice. They got into a conversation and Bull gave Hills a long dissertation on what was wrong with the *Herald*, why it was losing money and what could be done to set it right. Undoubtedly the liquor had affected Hills' judgment, because he suddenly asked Bull if he would like to become city editor. Needless to say, Bull accepted immediately. The two of them then repaired to the *Herald* office and Hills announced to Allen Finn, the present city editor, that he was to be replaced by Bull the next day. Finn was stunned and so was everyone else.

Bull's reputation had been permanently affected by a story he had produced when he was a rewrite man for the *Tribune*. He was given a routine story that had come in from the British Embassy about the dedication by the Prince of Wales of an orphanage for children of British soldiers who had served in France. Bull was told to liven the story up a little. He did, by creating a scene in which the Prince, inspecting the orphanage, stopped to ask a little boy how he liked his new home. "What the hell do you care, you rich son-of-a-bitch?" the child said. And Bull, in the throes of inspiration, added, "Whereupon the Prince hauled off and gave the tyke a belt with his swagger-stick."

Somehow this story was actually printed in the *Tribune*. The result was to be expected: Bull was fired. Now he sat before me as editor of the *Herald* and I had to give him my Roosevelt copy. "There's one of the best political stories of the year," I said, trying to be funny.

He read it and looked up at me. "He'll never make it," he said. "The American people will never put a cripple in the White House."

By the time I left his office a cold wind had sprung up, blowing rain in great gusts through the streets. In front of the hotel across the rue de Berri a uniformed porter, huddled under a small, lop-sided umbrella, was frantically trying to summon a taxi by blowing a whistle. I turned up the collar of my coat and headed for the Champs Élysées, but I was forced to stop and take shelter under a café awning: it flapped wildly, making loud popping noises. I waved at taxis; eventually one stopped at the curb near me to discharge a passenger. I rushed across the pavement and dived headlong into its shelter. The taxi slithered into the black sheen of the Champs, narrowly missing a fast-moving coupe.

We crossed the Seine over the beautiful Pont Alexandre III. The Waringtons lived in an apartment house in the fashionable and expensive district near the Chambre des Deputés. Mrs Warington opened the door to me. She was a small woman; her white hair was rolled in a chignon, and she smelled of lilacs. She said that Patricia was dressing and would be out presently. The living room was impressive: it contained a grand piano and paintings by El Greco and Holbein. Large French windows led onto a terrace; one could see Des Invalides and even Sacré Coeur. We sat down and Mrs Warington said, "Patricia has been telling me about you. She was very complimentary."

"I'm glad to hear that," I said. "Ever since I met her I've been trying to court her."

Mrs Warington smiled. "I'm afraid you're wasting your time," she said. "She's going to marry someone else."

"So I understand. I'm hoping to talk her out of it."

"I'm afraid she's made up her mind," she said. She stood up. "Can I get you a drink?"

"Don't you agree she's making a mistake? How old is the fellow?"

"You do ask a lot of questions," she said. Her smile had frozen a little. "He's forty-eight. Can I get you a drink?"

"Forty-eight," I said. "My Lord!"

"He's a member of one of France's oldest families. Would you like a brandy?"

"Thanks," I said. "Is it important about his family?"

"Patricia thinks it is," she said. She poured a brandy from a decanter on a silver tray near her.

"I suppose he's a Catholic," I said. "If the marriage doesn't work she'll be stuck."

Mrs Warington sat up very straight, with her hands folded in her lap. "I don't think you ought to worry about that," she said.

I sipped the brandy. "It's the classic story," I said. "American girl marries titled poor man."

Mrs Warington had stopped smiling. "I think the Count has some money," she said. "He has servants, and the family owns property at Avignon."

"Where are they going to live?"

"Don't you think you've asked enough questions?" she said. "I suppose even a newspaperman ought to know when to stop."

"I'm terribly sorry," I said. "I didn't mean to be rude."

"Didn't you?" she asked. At that point Patricia came in. She was wearing dark blue silk pyjamas; her hair was coiled in braids around her head. "Sorry I'm late," she said. "I hope you and mother hit it off." She poured herself a pony of brandy.

"Please excuse me," Mrs Warington said stiffly. She left the room.

"We've been discussing your upcoming mistake," I said.

"You mean my marriage," Patricia said. She refilled both our glasses.

"Your marriage. My sorrow."

She laughed musically, apparently enjoying the conversation. "Folderol!" she said.

"Folderol my foot! Why don't you marry someone your own age, someone you have something in common with? Someone like me?"

"I have a better idea," she said. Her eyes glinted with amusement. "I'll marry Charles and I'll take you as my lover."

"That's not a bad idea," I said. "When do we start?"

"Let me see. After the wedding, of course. It's set for the nineteenth, at the mairie of the seventh arondissement. You're invited, by the way."

"Oh, good," I said. "I wouldn't want to miss that." I finished the brandy. "But I'm going to waste a wish now. I wish you wouldn't do it." I looked at her earnestly. "A forty-eight-year-old man! He hasn't got much left to give, and he hasn't got that long to live, really."

"Ah," she said, laughing. She tucked herself into a corner of the sofa. "I'm marrying him for affection and companionship."

"Don't forget his title," I said. I offered her a Gauloise,

but she took an American cigarette from a silver box on the table next to her.

"I haven't," she said, blowing smoke toward the ceiling. "You'll have to call me Madame la Comtesse." She drew on the cigarette again. "It'll be fun being a countess."

Shortly afterward the maid announced dinner. Mrs Warington cast something of a pall over the atmosphere at the table; it was clear that I had managed to irritate her. But somehow the subject of my mother came up, and it turned out that Mrs Warington was an astrology buff. She knew my mother's magazine, and her manner softened considerably.

I told the two women about Legs Diamond; I had started a story about him called "Trial Without Jury". "Poor guy," I said. "I think he went through life thinking laws just didn't apply to him. He thought he could take whatever he wanted. But I liked him a lot."

"It sounds like a good story," Patricia said. "Doesn't it, Mother?"

"It could be," Mrs Warington said.

Patricia's wedding took place in the office of the mayor of the Comte's arondissement. It was of course a private wedding. On certain days the mayor of each arondissement married several couples en masse in his office. This would never do for the Comte de Rouselle. His wedding was a social event and since I was going to attend anyway, I offered to cover it for Eva Brown, the *Herald's* society editor.

I got to the mairie early, and waited outside for the principals to arrive, which they did eventually in a taxi. The Count got out first, and attempted to help Patricia and her mother to follow him; at the same time he appeared anxious to pay the driver before the meter chalked up another fifty centimes. In the resultant confusion Mrs

Warington lost her footing and fell against the Marquis de Chambrun, the best man, whose silk hat fell into the gutter. The Count was a man of medium height, with rather short legs and a puffy pink face. He wore an obvious toupee. His coat tails nearly touched the ground, and he wore a bright purple handkerchief in his breast pocket.

The procession into the mairie, past the concierge's glass-paneled door, was witnessed by a deeply impressed gendarme, and a street cleaner who leaned on his broom and watched, open-mouthed.

I followed the party up the stairs to the first floor where a man stood, imposingly arrayed in knee breeches and a long, braided coat. He wore a puggaree, and held in both hands a staff topped with a large silver knob. The Count approached him, identified himself and gave the purpose of his visit. The attendant responded, bowing, and led us to a large square room. Against the red-papered walls hung gold-framed portraits of heroes of the French Revolution. We seated ourselves on fragile gilt chairs with red plush seats, the Count on one side of Patricia and I on the other, next to the Marquis. "There's something barbaric about marriage ceremonies," Patricia said, breaking the awkward silence.

The Marquis chuckled briefly. "It's so deucedly hard to stay married after one goes to all the trouble," he said. "People of the upper classes shouldn't have to marry; it's too common. *And* too expensive." He leaned forward and looked at the Count, who responded with a nervous laugh and a glance at Patricia from the corners of his red-rimmed eyes.

Presently the attendant reappeared and opened a pair of wide double doors. We rose and followed him once more into an auditorium where rows of chairs faced a raised platform on which was a high desk draped with a

French flag. We seated ourselves in the front row of chairs, after which the mayor himself entered: a dignified white-haired man with a heavy silver chain around his neck.

"Bonjour, Messieurs, 'dames." He bowed slightly and sat down behind the desk.

We all responded "Bonjour, Monsieur," in ragged chorus.

The mayor then spent some moments studying papers, no doubt impressing on his mind the names of the bride and groom. We sat motionlessly waiting; I couldn't help feeling that I was on trial for a felony. The mayor put down his papers and requested that the bride and groom rise, which they did, with much cracking of bones on Charles' part. They were then subjected to a long speech concerning the joys and sorrows of marriage, the dangers and delights of passion and the importance of fidelity. God was not mentioned. The mayor said that trust, faith and fidelity were the qualities by which marriage survived.

After the happy couple were united in wedlock, the attendant went through the assembly carrying a collection box and chanting, "Pour le pauvres! Pour les pauvres!" I assumed the collection was really for the poor; the mayor, I had been told, had been paid in advance. After the box was withdrawn the mayor descended to the floor of the auditorium, shook hands with the newly-weds, asked them to sign their names, wished them good luck and everlasting happiness, and retired.

We went directly to the Warington apartment, where the Count and Countess were going to live; Mrs Warington had found other accommodations. The Count's servants, Ambrose and Nana, were there; he apparently had no living relatives. Ambrose and Nana had been in

Dinner party at the Waringtons

the service of the Count's parents and now he had in-
herited them. They were both very old and thin, and
quite deaf. Ambrose was French and spoke little English,
and Nana was English and spoke almost no French. Mrs
Warington showed them the tiled kitchen with its electric
stove and hanging copper pans; they were almost overcome with surprise and delight.

Piled in the hall were suitcases, valises and boxes in
various states of decrepitude; as it turned out most of
them were the property of Ambrose and Nana. Mrs. Warington's hopes had been rasied too high: the Count's
possessions consisted of his title and his two ancient servants.

As I left the party I congratulated Patricia again, and
kissed her cheek. "When do we start our affair?" I
whispered.

She laughed and put her finger to her lips. "One thing
at a time," she said.

VIII
Visiting Firemen:
Charlie Chaplin, Walter
Houston and Others

Among the famous people I interviewed in Paris was Charlie Chaplin. I wrote to Mother about him in a tone that was not exactly enchanted:

> The past week I have been occupied with Charles Spencer Chaplin. Thank heaven he left yesterday for the Riviera. He has come to Europe to promote his new film *City Lights* and all Paris is agog over his visit. I was at the railway station when he arrived. Since the French and apparently everyone else adore him, it was bedlam: hundreds of people of all ages had gathered to greet him; he was mobbed when he got off the train. Four men had to carry him over their heads to a limousine. I was with Lacy Kastner, the European head of United Artists, who are distributing the film, and we rode with him to the Hôtel Crillon, where hundreds more had congregated to get a look at him.
>
> The Crillon has a balcony which overlooks the Place de la Concorde, and Chaplin came out on it to

wave to the multitude and throw kisses to them. He acted as though he were a king. I thought it was kind of ridiculous, but tears were actually running down the faces of many people in the crowd. He has obviously given great pleasure to many, but I have developed an allergy to any kind of hero worship ever since the Lindbergh madness.

Lacy Kastner told me that Chaplin was getting ten million francs, or $400,000, for the film's first-run rights in Paris at one theatre, the largest in the city. The owner of the theatre had taken a big gamble in agreeing to pay that much money, so for promotion purposes to help insure his investment, he had used his clout to have Chaplin made a member of the Legion of Honor. Chaplin himself was greatly impressed by this, and wore the chevalier red ribbon in his lapel. The Legion of Honor still makes good publicity, but otherwise it is worth very little here anymore. I know it impresses Americans, but in Paris it seems sometimes that everyone and his brother is wearing that red ribbon. I know this sounds cynical and you won't like my saying it, but I think the honor can be bought.

During my interview with Chaplin, he talked at great length about the devaluation of the British pound. You probably know that its value has been cut in half. No doubt Chaplin considers himself a monetary expert, and his opinion is probably justified, judging from the fees he is collecting. He spent the better part of an hour telling me what is wrong with the world economy. I took scrupulous notes and wrote up the story as a kind of mock movie scenario but the managing editor, Eric Hawkins, would not run it. He said readers would not appreciate any attempt to make fun of their beloved Charlie, and I had to rewrite the thing in a more conventional style.

Charlie Chaplain in "City Lights"

I saw *City Lights,* and I really enjoyed it. But I think I prefer Chaplin's classic two-reelers. He used to film, cut, title and release one about every three weeks. Today producing seven reels takes him as long as two years and costs a million dollars or more. He does not work as quickly, and so the public must pay more to see his films. I asked him about talking pictures which are the latest craze, and he said he did not want to get involved with them, because his films are shown all over the world and he wants them to be comprehensible in any language.

So much for Mr Chaplin. I sent my Legs Diamond story to Jean Wick. She writes that its quality is saleable, but it may be too long (it is ten thousand words) and "may not be sufficiently fictionalized for some markets."

The entertaining of visiting firemen was—and probably still is—one of the minor annoyances for Americans living in Paris. Hardly a week passed during the tourist season that someone didn't come to see me with a letter of introduction from relatives, friends, or casual acquaintances. Sometimes the letter bearer was hardly known to the author. "Going to Paris? I tell you what. Look up old so-and-so. He'll show you the town."

Speed Denlinger, a friend of mine on the *New York World-Telegram,* had sent me one such visitor. Her name was Rhea Gore Huston, and Speed had met her at a party and told her to look me up. Rhea had been working for the *New York Graphic,* a yellow sheet, and had come to Paris to get another newspaper job. I took her to my favorite restaurant on the rue Jacob for chateaubriands and a bottle of Côte de Rhone rouge. While we ate she talked incessantly about her son, John, and his father, an actor named Walter Huston, of whom I had never heard.

She told me how she and Walter had met in 1904 in St Louis where she was a theatrical reporter and he was performing in *The Sign of the Cross.*

"I watched the show and when I went backstage to interview the star," she said, "I ran into this handsome young man. I didn't remember having seen him on stage and I asked if he was in the show. He said he was; he played the old Christian, he said, the fellow with the whiskers who carries the staff. I couldn't believe it. I said, 'You mean that old man was *you?* I'd have never known it.'

"We went to an ice cream parlor. I told him I wanted to write plays and he was very encouraging. After that we saw each other almost every day for the rest of the summer, while the show was in town. We went to the World's Fair, we roller-skated, bicycled, visited penny arcades and had our fortunes told. The gypsy told me that I was going to marry a rich man and have five children, and that I was going to be famous. Well, Walter wasn't rich, and we had only one child—John. And I never became famous— but Walter did."

"Is Walter here with you?" I asked.

"Oh, no. We were divorced long ago."

She was not really interested in talking about Walter; she much preferred talking about John. A book he had written based on the folk song "Frankie and Johnny" had recently been published with illustrations by Miguel Covarrubias, a relatively obscure Mexican artist; she considered this one of the important literary events of all time. She felt that writing was only one of John's talents; she was confident he would make a strong mark in the world.

I had never heard a doting parent brag so shamelessly; I was bored to distraction. I certainly did not believe

that anyone—with the possible exception of myself—
could be as lavishly talented as Rhea Huston insisted her
son was. I could not even break into her encomium to tell
her about the book I had recently finished. When I finally
did mention it she did not respond; I could not be sure
whether she heard me. She just went on talking about
John.

Despite her lack of interest in me, I gave her the
names of some people who might be able to help her get a
job. But she was not successful and after a relatively brief
time she went back to New York. I did not see her again,
but I did meet John Huston, who *was* singularly talented
and used his talents in motion pictures; he and I eventually became close friends. In fact I was with him in California on the day his mother died.

I wrote to Mother about Rhea Huston and asked her if
she herself spent a lot of time extolling my virtues to people. I was relieved when she replied that when she spoke
of me she tended to be complimentary, but brief.

Another visiting fireman that spring was Maxwell
Bodenheim, the author of *Replenishing Jessica* and
Georgia May, among other novels. I had known Max in
Greenwich Village: we had both lived in the same apartment house on Barrow Street. He had been born in
Mississippi and had pink eyes. He came to look me up at
the paper almost as soon as he arrived in Paris. He was in
financial difficulties. He had come to Europe with a girl
he met in Barney Gallant's in Greenwich Village and she
had deserted him in Antwerp, taking most of his money.

"Do you know where she went?" I asked.

"Capri. With a woman she met on the ship. I think
she's a lesbian."

"Who? The woman?"

"No, my girl. Maybe both. I never was any good at
judging females. She was fun to be with and she was all

right in bed. I liked her a lot. In fact, I was thinking of
marrying her."

"Well, it's a blessing you found out in time, isn't it?"

"Yes, but it's demeaning to have a dame walk out on
you, especially after you've paid her way over here. It
doesn't help your ego one bit."

"You're supposed to be an expert on female psychology."

His pink eyes gazed sadly at me. "There ain't one," he
said. "Not even Kraft-Ebbing."

He was staying with me until he could get some
money. That night we went to the Trianon because Max
was almost desperately eager to meet James Joyce and the
Joyces sometimes dined at the Trianon. He wasn't there
that night, but Ludwig Lewisohn was, and I introduced
them. Max was overjoyed to meet another Jewish writer.
During dinner Max told me about *Naked on Roller Skates*,
a novel he had just finished. He was immersed in socialist
thought and kept talking about Sacco and Vanzetti. The
trial and the appeals had gone on for years and Max,
along with many intellectuals, believed the two men had
really been executed for political reasons.

As we were leaving the restaurant, Max went ahead
while I paid the check. An American acquaintance of
mine who had been sitting at a nearby table took me
aside. "Say," he whispered, "who is that fellow you're
with?"

I told him.

"Well," he said, "he sounds pretty fishy to me.
Whatever he's trying to sell, don't buy it."

As soon as we reached the street Max said, "What did
that guy want?"

"He wanted to know who you were," I said tactfully. "I
told him you're a famous writer."

"I didn't like his looks."

A few days later Max left for Capri.

Remembering Max reminds me of a couple of other similar types I knew in Paris. One was Harold Stearns. Harold was an intellectual who talked well, sometimes brilliantly, but lacked self-confidence and never really accomplished much. He had been the shining light of the *New Republic* but he felt New York was too confining for a person of his talents, and so he came to Paris. He worked for a while on the *Herald,* but he was not an easy person to get on with and he was fired. Then be became obsessed with horse racing and made daily racing selections for the *Tribune* under the arch name of Peter Pickem. That job didn't last long either and after that he spent most of his time cadging food and drink from whomever he could, before making his way back to New York.

Another poseur was Mike Romanoff, who had been born in Brooklyn, and claimed to be a Russian prince. He had only one talent, and that was charm, and he had plenty of it. He could turn it on whenever he needed it. He became something of a minor celebrity in Paris because of his ability to eat and drink without spending any money. Newcomers found him entertaining and were happy to buy drinks for him. People who invited him to parties quickly learned what the old timers had long known: he was adhesive, difficult to remove. He had no permanent address and slept wherever he happened to be. I don't know where he kept his few belongings—I do know that he always carried a toothbrush and comb. He turned up at my place shortly after I met him, saying that he wanted to take a bath. He did, and stayed with me for more than a week. When he found another host, he left, remarking that what he had really appreciated about his stay with me was being able to get his laundry done.

Montparnasse swarmed with Americans who lived on

stipends sent from home. They were supposed to be working on artistic or literary projects, but the vast majority of them spent most of their time sitting at sidewalk cafés, drinking Pernods, talking endlessly, and watching the world go by. There were notable exceptions, of course. One was Alexander Calder, who lived in my neighborhood. He was a plump young man, seven years older than I, who had studied engineering in college but had come to Paris to paint, having been influenced by the work of Joan Miró.

I went to a party at his place once. The first things I noticed were several wire and metal chip concoctions hanging from the ceiling. He seemed very proud of them: they were in motion, and he said they were a new form of sculpture. I thought he was pretty childish. And this opinion was reinforced by the entertainment he provided his guests: a miniature circus. No one in his right mind, I thought, could expect this kind of nonsense to be accepted as art. I believed that Calder needed psychiatric help. These concoctions were of course the first of Calder's "mobiles", the name suggested by Marcel Duchamp. It never entered my head that anyone would ever even look at them, let alone take them seriously. That was not the first time my crystal ball was clouded.

IX

The Contessa, a Duel
and Joyce Again

After the wedding I thought a good deal about the new Countess. She and Charles spent their honeymoon on the Riviera. Weeks went by, and I decided that I had better put her out of my mind for good.

But one never knows what each day will bring, and one listless afternoon Patricia called me at the office. I was overwhelmed with surprise and delight. The next day was my day off and we arranged to meet at La Closerie des Lilas, just down the avenue Montparnasse from my lodgings.

When I got there, she was already sitting in a far corner. She was more beautiful than ever. Her smile was radiant, as warming as sunshine. I sat down, and we held hands across the table.

"I'm ecstatic to see you," I said. "I thought you had gone out of my life forever."

"I'm back."

"How goes the marriage?"

She shrugged. "Fine," she said. "I'm getting along all right. It's a big adjustment for me."

"I warned you," I said.

"Mother has found an apartment near the Étoile," she said. "I rather miss her. And then. . . you keep popping up in my dreams."

"You pop up in mine," I said. "What happens when I pop up?"

"It's frustrating," she said.

"Mine are the same. But there's a way we can overcome that."

She got up. "Let's go for a walk," she said.

We strolled to the Jardin du Luxembourg and sat on a bench near the pool, watching the children sail their toy boats.

She said that Charles was a gentleman in every sense of the word: courteous and erudite. However, he had never worked in his life and he hung around the apartment all day. As for the two old servants, Nana and Ambrose, they were simply a nuisance. "They don't take care of me," she said. "I take care of them."

Clover was growing at our feet. "I think I'll look for a four-leafer," I said, "to bring good luck."

She laughed. "I tell you what," she said. "If you can find a four-leaf clover, we just might be able to resolve our frustration."

I leapt up and knelt in the grass. "In that case," I said, "I'll stay here and find one if it takes two days."

But in a very short time I did find one, and then I found six more.

We went to my quarters.

It was a glorious experience. When the time came I offered to take her home. "Better not," she said. "Charles is extremely jealous of you."

After that she came to my place on my days off, and stayed for the afternoon. Those were the only times we could see each other. She told Charles that she was taking art lessons. After a few months he began to ask her how she was progressing. He said he was surprised that she never brought any work home to show him. She put him off: she would show him her work when she felt it really showed sufficient progress, she said. In the meantime she was not sure she had any talent.

One afternoon Patricia and I were sitting in my rooms having tea, both fully dressed, when there was a knock at the door. I got up, opened it and was dumbfounded to face Charles. Behind him stood a tall, swarthy fellow with fierce moustaches.

"Well," I said. "Well, well! Hello, Charles." I tried to pull myself together. "Please come in. You're just in time for tea."

Charles pushed past me without answering. The fierce moustache followed him and, kicking the door shut with his heel, stood against it with his arms folded.

"Is this your art school?" Charles said to Patricia.

Her face was very white, but she answered calmly. "Of course it isn't. Actually I've just come from there."

"I happen to know that you did nothing of the sort. You came straight here from home." He indicated the moustaches. "This person is a detective; he has been following you."

"Really, Charles!" she said. It was probably all she could think of to say, and I couldn't think of anything either.

"What are you doing here?" Charles said.

"I was invited to tea."

He scooped up her coat from the settee. "Well, you're coming home right now." He was trembling with rage.

"Why are you so upset?" Patricia asked. She was gearing up to go on the offensive.

"I don't like being lied to."

She snatched her coat from him. "There's nothing more innocent than a tea party," she said. "You're being very rude."

Charles turned his attention to me. His normally pink face was red, and his round chin was quivering. "As for you," he said, "you are a damned soul." He turned sharply and pushed Patricia toward the door, which the silent detective quickly opened. Charles turned back on the threshold and shook his finger at me. "You will hear from me!" he said with venom.

"It'll be a pleasure," I said, in a wretched attempt at wit.

"The hell it will," he responded. And they were gone.

I missed Patricia terribly, and moped around the office. To cheer me up Elliot Paul suggested I go with him to a bordello he often visited. It was called Le Panier Fleuri and was on the rue de la Huchnette, a couple of doors away from his rooms. He was well known there, and called it the parlor of joy. I was not interested in any carnal activity, being most upset about Patricia, but Elliot went there mostly to amuse the girls by playing the concertina for them. Le Panier officially opened at two p.m. and closed at two a.m., so we went at noon. The lady in charge was named Madame Mariette; she was middle-aged and world-weary, expensively dressed, and wore a great bunch of keys on a chatalaine at her waist. She greeted us warmly and had a bottle of champagne fetched from her cellars. The girls were having breakfast when we arrived, but they came into the parlor soon afterward: seven of them; one was a black woman from Martinique. They were not offered any champagne. Elliot played songs everybody knew, including "Mademoiselle from Armentières" and we all sang.

While we were enjoying the music a doctor arrived; his name was Clouet, and he came every day to examine the girls who were enjoined by law from engaging in business without his imprimatur. He stayed in the parlor for a while after his examinations to share the champagne and general merriment. He left with Elliot and me before the first customer arrived.

I did other things to forget about my distressing experience with Patricia's husband. Paris was filled with White Russians who had fled there after the Revolution; I had two Russian friends who invited me to accompany them to the Easter services at the Russian Church of Paris. Services began on Saturday night at ten o'clock and continued until noon on Easter Sunday, which is one week later than the non-Orthodox Easter. We arrived at ten o'clock on Saturday night at the magnificent church, built with minarets and domes. The interior was empty space, devoid of seats or pews, but it was packed with people, including children. We could barely squeeze our way in. We stood for three hours during the service. For about half the time we listened to a reading in Latin of the story of the crucifixion and resurrection. Three men took turns reading from a large gilded book; while the reading went on a procession of mostly elderly men and women moved along, waiting to kneel and kiss something before the altar.

The church was lighted by three gigantic electrified chandeliers and electric sconces set at intervals in the walls. The white tallow candles which blazed on the altar were continually replaced by women with white scarves over their hair. In the ceiling of the central dome was a painting of Christ in a blue gown, with outstretched arms.

When the reading ended a procession came from the large vestibule behind the altar: first came four young boys carrying tall candles; then four priests in brocade robes and golden headpieces, followed by priests dressed in wine-red robes, and lastly, men in evening dress carrying pictures of Jesus as a child and a young man. They worked their way through the massed devotees and out through the great doors of the church; we could not see them, then, but we could hear their voices chanting, full and resonant. There was no music. Everyone around me crossed himself at each pause in the song. The heat was oppressive and so was the body contact. I was pushed so close to a woman next to me that I thought of the joke about the man on the crowded subway who, on leaving, handed his card to the girl mashed up against him and said, "Here's my name in case anything comes of this."

At a few minutes after one in the morning, I was suffering from heat and exhaustion. I said good-night to my friends and literally fought my way out into the delicious cool air. Hundreds of people milled about before the church. I took a taxi to the Dôme—the last Metro train had left some time before—where the atmosphere on the terrace was one of laughter and drink. I had a fleeting urge to join them, but I was too tired even for that. I went home to bed, quite worn out by the grandeur of my experience.

The next day when I got home from work the concierge handed me a note. It was from Comte Charles de Rouselle:

You have insulted and humiliated me. I challenge you to a duel with foils. Be at the Porte d'Anteuil Saturday at six a.m. I will bring the foils. I await a reply.

My first reaction was that it must be a joke. Charles couldn't be serious. It was such a pompous, antiquated thing! Besides, he was old and fat. I did not see how he could expect to carry through. I had learned fencing from John Barrymore when I was a stunt man in Hollywood; he had taught me the fundamentals. And I was a pretty good athlete. In any case it was a dangerous kind of sport; one of us could be hurt—maybe both of us. I really wanted to ignore this ridiculous challenge, but I couldn't accept the idea that Charles would be all over the place telling people that I was a coward. I was young enough to hate that idea.

I told Elliot Paul about it. He said he was sure Charles was serious. "It's against the law," he said, "but the police don't really give a damn. It goes on here, and I guess this guy really wants to hurt you."

"He may want to kill me," I said.

"Oh, no. That would be ungentlemanly. All he wants to do is carve his initials on your belly." I didn't think that was very funny. "I'd offer to serve as your second, but I can't get up at that ungodly hour. The only one who is up—besides roosters—is Sparrow Robertson. Why don't you ask him? I bet he'll do it so he can get an item out of it for his column."

I decided to follow his advice. Sure enough, Sparrow agreed.

About five-thirty on Saturday morning I engaged a taxicab driven by a Russian named Igbagnatchev, with a bushy red beard and pale gray eyes. We picked Sparrow up at the *Herald* office. I was a nervous wreck; Sparrow was in fine fettle although he had not been to bed at all that night. We drove a little way in the gloom and Sparrow spotted a bistro sign. "Say," he said, "how about some coffee to warm us up?"

It was a chilly dawn. The driver pulled up before the bistro, where a man in a blue apron was sweeping the sidewalk with a homemade broom. Sparrow always said hello to everybody. "Bonjour, pal," he said. The man did not respond. The zinc bar was crowded with men who had stopped off on their way to work. Everyone was drinking café fin. I gulped mine down, and then began to get restless. Sparrow went to the toilet. After about five minutes I followed him and called to him through the door to hurry up.

"Keep your shirt on," he said. "A gentleman of breeding should always keep his dueling opponent waiting."

We got under way again. The streets were damp with early morning mist, which dripped from the budding trees. Gradually buildings along the Champs Élysée were emerging from the darkness. There was very little traffic; a squat green streetcar slipped past us, almost empty. At the Porte d'Auteuil was parked a large shiny limousine. "Pull up beside it," I said to the Russian. I got out of the cab and looked into the open window of the back seat. Charles, wearing a top hat and overcoat, with a white silk muffler around his neck, was sitting with the Marquis de Chambrun.

"Good morning," I said, with forced cheerfulness.

"You're late," Charles said. "Please tell your driver to follow us."

I got back into the taxi and we followed the limousine down a road leading into the woods. We stopped in a secluded area surrounded by tall pines. Everyone got out of the cars, including the chauffeurs. The scene was unreal. "I think it's too foggy to fence," Sparrow observed.

I went up to Charles, who was removing his overcoat. "I beg your pardon," I said politely, "but I would like to know the rules of this game. I know how we begin, but when do we stop?"

"When you are unable to continue," Charles said. He handed his overcoat to the Marquis and began to remove his jacket.

"We're not going to try to kill each other, are we?" He looked at me with contempt. "When the first blood is drawn, that will be the winning sign."

Sparrow came up to us. "Come on, gents," he said. "Let's get on with it. I'm freezing."

The Marquis turned away to get the foils. "One more thing," I said to Charles, trying to lighten the atmosphere, "Sparrow Robertson is my manager as well as my second, and he won't permit me to proceed unless he is guaranteed the newspaper rights."

"I suggest you treat this matter with some seriousness," Charles said. He took the foils from the Marquis and, holding the blades with his left hand, presented their handles to me over his right arm. I hurried out of my jacket, tossed it to Sparrow, and then chose one of the foils. It consisted of a long steel blade with a quadrangular section and a light metal handle in the shape of a figure eight backed with a piece of stiff leather. Charles walked away and turned to stand facing me, balancing the point of his weapon on the toe of his right shoe. I assumed that was the proper stance, and imitated it.

"Are you ready, gentlemen?" the Marquis asked. "On guard!" We raised our foils. "Go!"

Charles feinted at once, and I parried. He lunged forward with surprising agility thrusting at my chest; I parried with a high prime. He withdrew quickly and riposted. My salvation obviously depended on defense, so I kept parrying, trying to keep him off balance. He moved with extreme dexterity. The clash of metal in the silent

A duel

grove was a chilling sound. I made a long thrust; he backed up and riposted so quickly that he barely missed my face. I didn't try that again. After awhile I noticed to my relief that he was perspiring heavily. But he showed no signs of slowing up; indeed, he increased his pace if anything, thrusting and riposting, and I had to use every ounce of wit and all my youthful agility to keep ahead of him.

"You've done this before," I gasped, still trying to mollify him.

"I have," he said, still coldly.

"You're very good. . ."

"Merde!"

I could hear the chauffeurs arguing about which of us would win. The Russian had the louder voice. I didn't dare even attempt to turn my head to look at them. The fog lifted; the day had begun. The clash of the foils continued: thrust, parry, riposte, recoil. I was growing very tired, and I could see that Charles was tiring too. His thrusts were not as swift and frequent. His always pink face was very red and he was breathing rapidly through his open mouth. "You can stop whenever you like," I said hopefully.

"Not until I draw blood," he said through clenched teeth, and he began another flurry. But soon it diminished. We had been fencing for at least fifteen minutes. Presently it became obvious that we were merely going through the motions.

"Why don't you gentlemen stop this foolishness?" Sparrow said.

Igbagnatchev said something in Russian which suggested that we should make friends.

Suddenly Charles stepped back and lowered his foil.

He did not speak, but his eyes looked like the eyes of a stricken deer. His attitude seemed to say: Go on, stab me. I have lost.

I lowered my weapon also. "Is that it?" I asked.

He did not answer. "I think that it is over," the Marquis said. "My friend's honor is satisfied."

"Permit me to apologize for offending you," I said formally to Charles.

He grunted and wiped his face with a white handkerchief. "Where did you learn to fence like that?" he asked.

"In Hollywood," I said. "I was a stunt man."

His bulging eyes studied my face for a moment. "You surprise me," he said.

We began to put on our jackets. "Let's go get a drink," Sparrow said, and the Marquis laughed. "Spoken like a true gentleman," he said.

Sparrow's account of the contest did not identify the contestants:

> One of my new pals was challenged to a duel by a titled gentleman whom he had inexplicably insulted. I went along as his second. The foiling was done among the fallen leaves of the Bois de Boulogne the other morning before the cocks began to crow. It was a contest to behold and went on until both adversaries got petered. Neither of the gentlemen won or was injured and in the end they kissed and made up. We all went to a fashionable saloon, had a champagne peace party and got plastered. It was great fun.

Of course the gossips found out who had been involved in this affair and why. I got flack from my confreres. The whole episode was ludicrous, and it ended my affair with Patricia. She wrote to me telling me that the Count no longer wished to remain in Paris; this was farewell, she said, but she would love me forever. She drew a circle around an ink splotch on the paper and identified it as a tear.

Shortly afterward she and Charles moved to Juan-les-Pins. The last time I heard of her I was told she was having an affair with a dentist.

I wrote Mother about the duel and went on:

> Have not heard from Jean Wick about my novel, but I am hard at work on my second. It's about my experiences in Hollywood, and I'm calling it *Men Are April When They Woo* from Shakespeare's *As You Like It.* I've been reading Thomas Mann's *Magic Mountain* and I can't recommend it to you too strongly. It is magnificent. Nine hundred pages, 350,000 words. Marvelous characters: Hans Castorp, Settembrini, Naptha the Jesuit. Filled with arguments attacking and defending religion, corporal and capital punishment, science, ethics. . . all tremendously interesting. Some paragraphs stand out like pyramids. In one long passage Hans Castorp delves into medicine and science to try to find an explanation for the miracle of life. After long research through difficult phases of medicine, through the examination of the body by x-ray, through the mind in the light of reason, one reaches the bottom of the big pot and there is the answer: life consists of water, salt, albumen, sugar and starch.
>
> I really urge you to read it.
>
> Yesterday I happened to sit with James Joyce and his wife at the Dôme and I mentioned *The Magic*

James Joyce

Mountain to him. I told him I thought he was the only man alive besides Thomas Mann who could understand it all. Mann dips into many languages, ancient and modern—what a task it must have been for the translators! Of course it was written originally in German and in the foreward the translator thanks three specialists for their help.

Joyce had not read it; he said he couldn't afford to buy new books. So I went and got mine to lend to him. Although his eyesight is bad, he manages avidly to read works in at least seven languages. He works with intensity. He told me it took him fifteen years to write *Finnegan's Wake,* and when I mentioned that to Elliot Paul, Elliot said it would take at least that long to read it. Big joke.

I gather that Joyce's only income is from the sale of *Ulysses.* Fortunately it sells well here, although it is banned in the U.S. Or maybe because it is banned: tourists buy it to sneak it home. It sells for five dollars and I'm told he gets one dollar for each five. That's a lot for an author, since as you know the usual royalty is ten to fifteen percent. His fame is growing here, thanks particularly to *Ulysses.* I don't know how well he is known in America. A reviewer wrote in *The New York Times* that '*Ulysses* will immortalize its author with the same certainty that *Gargantua* immortalized Rabelais and *The Brothers Karamazov* immortalized Dostoievsky . . . It comes nearer the revelation of a personality than any book in existence.'

Joyce is gracious to aspiring writers; it is a pleasure to talk with him. I always come away feeling encouraged. I told him I was having a hard time finding a publisher for my novel and he said that he had always had difficulty getting his work published, even in his native Ireland. He praised Sylvia Beach, the American bookseller here who bravely paid to have *Ulysses* published, 'thus saving the manuscript from possible extinction.' Everybody needs an angel, he said. I am now avidly searching for one.

I guess some people are born to be famous: Joyce for example, and Sinclair Lewis and Scott Fitzgerald. Maybe it doesn't have that much to do with talent. It's in our stars.

X
Another Lady in Distress

That spring another visiting firewoman came armed with a letter of introduction, this one from my double-first cousin, Helene Coudray. Helene's father and mine were brothers and our mothers were sisters, so we felt like brother and sister. I'll call the visiting firewoman Susan Mann. I was out of the office when she came up with the letter so I telephoned her later at the Hôtel Université to welcome her to Paris. I suggested that we have breakfast the next morning at Aux Deux Magots. "It's just up the street from your hotel," I said. "Come about nine o'clock. You can recognize me because I'm twenty-five years old, six feet tall, one hundred sixty pounds, I have a Ronald Coleman moustache and I'll be wearing a brown tweed suit."

The next morning I picked up a *Herald* at the corner kiosk and walked down to the Deux Magots. I chose a table near a glowing brazier and ordered my usual coffee and croissant. It was just after nine o'clock. I was happy to see my interview with Jed Harris, the theatrical producer-director, prominently displayed on page three. I thought it was an amusing story and read well: he had greeted me at the door in the nude, his puckish face covered with lather and I had interviewed him in his bathroom while he finished shaving. I sipped my coffee and read on. I learned that a French woman had killed her faithless husband, that President Hoover was annoyed because France had not repaid her war debts, that ground had been broken in Posnan, Poland, for the Palace of Peace, which was to be the headquarters of the League of Nations. The huge entrance to the Palace was to be a memorial to Woodrow Wilson.

I had reached the sports page and it was twenty-five minutes after nine when a young woman entered the café. She was small and slight, had bobbed brown hair under a brown derby and wore a camel's hair coat. She spotted me at once.

"You must be John Weld," she said. "I'm so sorry I'm late. It's the difference in time. I see you're having breakfast. I'll have the same."

I called the waiter. Then I asked her about herself. She said she was twenty-two years old and was a secretary to a prominent lawyer in Washington, D.C., a truly wonderful man who had given her this trip to Europe.

I thought she was pretty young to be travelling all by herself in a strange country, and I said so. "Aren't you afraid?"

"Of what?"

"Oh, men. . . thieves. . . diseases. You look rather fragile, if you don't mind my saying so. You can't weigh more than a hundred pounds."

"Oh, I weigh one hundred and ten," she said. Her eye was caught by two young American men who seated themselves at a table near us. Both were wearing trench-

coats and felt hats with feathers in the bands and both
had shaven eyebrows. She looked at them with distaste.
The waiter brought her breakfast.

"I'm going to be here two, maybe three weeks," she
said. "I want to learn French."

"Well, that's not really enough time to learn French.
But you can go to the Alliance Française just up the street.
Didn't you study French in school?"

"Oh, yes, for two years." She broke her croissant and
buttered it. "About all I remember is 'bonjour'."

We were distracted by shouting from the street. Two
Americans I had met were playing leap-frog. One, a heavy
man, was a poet and the other, smaller one had come
from Virginia; he lived on a trust fund left him by his
father who had committed suicide. They were obviously
on their way home from their usual night on the town;
they spent most of their days in bed. Every time the small
one tried to leap over the fat one's back he got stuck,
sending them both into gales of laughter. As we watched,
the Virginian fell into the street and was narrowly missed
by a passing car. Two gendarmes stood on the sidewalk
watching them with tolerant amusement.

"Those fools will be killed," Susan said. "Whatever is
wrong with them?"

"I'm afraid they're drunk," I said.

We ate and drank in silence for a moment. Then she
leaned toward me across the table and lowered her voice.
"I'd like to talk to you privately," she said. "Not here. Could
we go to your place?"

I was rather startled. "Why, certainly," I said. "I live
just up the way.

"Oh, that would be fine."

The concierge at my place stopped scrubbing the
stairs and stood back so that we could pass him. We

climbed to the fourth landing. I unlocked the door with
the bludgeon of a key and stood aside so that she could
enter. I had a bed that did double duty as a couch, with
pillows for backrests, a partly-filled bookcase, two chairs,
a standing lamp and a card table with a typewriter on it. I
had bought the furniture from the former tenant.

"Oh, isn't this cute!" Susan said. She dropped her coat
on the divan and craned her neck to look at the books in
the bookcase. "I always say you can judge people by their
libraries," she said. I had stacks of *New Yorkers* and *This
Quarter*, a copy of the *American Mercury*, copies of Gor-
ky's *Bystander*, Douglas's *South Wind*, Gissing's *New Grub
Street*, Symons' *Lesbos*, Sackville-West's *The Edwardians*,
Joyce's *Ulysses*, of course, and a thesaurus and a couple of
dictionaries.

"Oh, and these etchings," she said. "I like them, but
they're very naughty."

"They're Willette's seven deadly sins," I said.

"What does 'luxure' mean?"

"Lust. And this is envy, and this is anger. . . Lazi-
ness. . . Pride. . . Stinginess. . . Greed. . ."

She was obviously reluctant to settle down and get to
the point.

"Why don't you sit down and tell me what's on your
mind?" I said.

She sat down on the one upholstered chair, crossed
her silk-hosed legs and fished in her handbag for a pack
of Chesterfields and a book of matches. "I hope you don't
mind if I smoke," she said.

"Of course not." I provided an ashtray, and then sat on
the divan. I thought she was attractive.

She leaned back and inhaled deeply, staring at the
ceiling. Then she exhaled and said abruptly, "I think I'm
pregnant. That's really why I'm here."

I was considerably taken aback. "It wouldn't be any problem if I were married," she said. "But I'm not. The. . . father of the child is a very important man, and he's married."

"Not Mr Hoover, I suppose," I said.

Her small chin quivered. "It's not funny, you know," she said. "I've got to have an abortion. Will you help me?"

"I don't know anything about it," I said. "How long has it been?"

"A couple of months."

"I suppose you've tried the usual?" I said. "Like jumping off tables? Or a hot bath?"

"I'd like to have it," she said. "I don't want to do this."

"Then," I said hopefully, "go ahead and have it if you want it."

Her eyes were filled with tears. "No, I can't. The scandal. It would be a beautiful baby. But it would ruin Walter. There's so much at stake."

I tried to think. "Look, the first thing you should do is see a doctor. I know a good one, if you haven't seen one yet."

"Will you go with me?"

I looked at my watch. I had some time before I had to go to work. It was only a little after eleven. And she couldn't speak French.

"All right, sure," I said. "Come on."

We walked down the boulevard Raspail on the sunny side where it was warmer. We passed the cinema near the rue de Rennes; *Our Blushing Brides* with Joan Crawford was playing there. Just beyond it, between shops, was the entrance to an arcade. I guided Susan into it and to a door with a brass plate: Georges Leclerq Docteur en médecine. I had consulted Dr Leclerq several times myself; I had met him when he examined Lindbergh.

"Just a minute," she said, as I put my hand on the knob.

She took a small compact from her bag. "I'm a wreck," she said. She put on powder and lipstick quickly. "There," she said, looking at me with an expectant smile. "Isn't that much better?"

She hadn't really been a wreck to start with, but I nodded gravely. "You look fine," I said.

Dr Leclerq greeted us. He had an abundant moustache and was tall and thin in his white smock. He held out his long, veined hand. I shook it, and introduced him to Susan.

"She's just arrived in Paris," I said, "and she has a problem. She's not feeling too well."

"I am enchanted to meet you, Mam'selle," he said. "If I can help. . ."

I patted her shoulder. "I've got to go to work," I said. "I'll talk to you later." He held his consulting room door open for her, and I left.

It was a pretty quiet day at the office so I took the opportunity to write Mother a letter filling her in on recent events:

> You probably know that the King and Queen of Spain, Alphonso XIII and Victoria, came to Paris last week, having fled Madrid in fear of their lives. They have abdicated the throne. Absolute hordes of people turned out to greet them here. It was extremely exciting; it's a kind of privilege to be caught in the sweep of history-making events like that—that is, if you don't get trampled to death!
>
> This was the real McCoy, a dramatic piece of history. Fortunately I was pushed by the mob quite close to the monarchs; indeed, they and I were actually swept along together. Alphonso is tall, slim and dark; Victoria is English, beautiful and dignified. I barked a few questions at them. Although they had just escaped with their lives, and were being herded

along like cattle—as we all were—they smiled and behaved very graciously.

I followed them to the Hotel Meurice where they have taken the top two storeys for themselves and their children and their entourage. They did not say where they plan to settle, but I guess it will be either England or Portugal. I don't know what is going to happen in Spain.

Yesterday I visited Rouen where a celebration is being held all this week in honor of Joan of Arc who was burned at the stake 500 years ago—in 1431. Rouen is charming: it is located on the Seine between Paris and Le Havre. During the war it was a British base—about a million men were stationed there, manufacturing guns and ammunition.

Part of the celebration was a pageant of French military history, starting with the Gauls. François I, Lafayette, Napoleon, the army in 1914—all in accurate costume. The French do these things really well; it was most impressive.

I rode back to Paris with the Commander of the local American Legion post—he's a dentist. He was driving a Packard, and we were going at a good clip— about seventy miles an hour. There was a lot of traffic on the Deauville road, and everyone was speeding. A Rolls Royce passed up as though we were riding a snail. It was as quiet too as an electric ice box . . .

At this point the phone rang. It was Susan. She said that Dr Leclerq had confirmed her pregnancy.

"He tried to talk me into having the baby and giving it up for adoption. Can you imagine? Having a child and then giving it to someone else? He had the nerve to say he could find a home for it with a nice American family. I should say not!"

"Was he any help at all?"

"Well, he gave me an address. A Madame Fournier. Apparently midwives do abortions here."

"Are you going to do it?"

"Yes, I'm going to do it! I have to. You'll come with me, won't you? I don't see how I could manage alone."

"Of course," I said stoutly. "We could do it tomorrow morning. Or tonight, if you want, after I get through work."

"I'd like it if we could go tonight." Her voice trembled a little. "I want to get it over with."

We met at the Deux Magots and set out at once for the address she gave me in the rue Bonaparte. She took my arm. "I know I'm imposing on you," she said. "I hate to do it, but you don't mind, do you? I'm in a hell of a fix."

"I'm only glad I can help," I said gallantly.

"You're very gallant," she said, echoing my own thought. She sighed. "There's something so romantic about Paris. Just think, kings and queens in their silks and satins have walked over these same stones. Have you ever thought about that?"

I said I had.

"Walter's forty-seven," she said. "He wants to get a divorce, you know, and marry me. He doesn't love his wife. But she's got a financial hold on him. It's an awful thing."

"You really should stop seeing him," I said. "Find yourself somebody who's free, so you can get married. You're on a dead end course." I felt self-conscious; I sounded like a Lonelyhearts columnist. The whole thing was right out of *True Confessions*.

"Oh, Walter and I love each other," she said confidently. "It's going to work out."

We turned into the rue Bonaparte. "I wish I were a

man," Susan said. "Men can live any way they like. Girls have an awful time, worrying about getting pregnant. Men can behave any way they want."

"Well," I said, "Not *any* way."

I rang the doorbell. After a moment the door was opened by a large woman with a grand bosom, who was drying her hands on a towel. She replied to my inquiry that she was indeed Madame Fournier, the "femme sage" and looked at Susan, who shrunk in her camel's hair coat, seemed smaller than ever.

I introduced Susan as Madame Smith and explained that she was pregnant. Could Madame Fournier possibly do anything for her?

Madame Fournier stood aside and invited us to enter her domain.

The salon was furnished in bad taste, and smelled musty; the French lower classes disliked opening windows. Susan and I sat down on a green velour sofa; Susan perched nervously on the edge of her cushion. The sage femme sat on a blue chair and began to talk in French so rapid that I could barely grasp the gist of what she was saying. She explained that an abortion is a difficult operation, and illegal to boot. For this reason it is expensive. Some femmes sage overcharge for the work, but she herself cheated no one. Her price was four thousand francs, payable in advance. She was an excellent practitioner, the best, as a matter of fact, in the country. If the price was agreeable to Madame and Monsieur, the operation could be performed the next day. It would take around two hours all told, and Susan could leave the premises almost immediately afterward.

It was agreed, and we all rose. Madame Fournier repeated that the money must be paid before the operation could be performed. I said I understood perfectly.

"Trés bien, monsieur," she said. "Merci, monsieur. Bonne nuit, monsieur, 'dame."

The next morning we returned. Susan was so nervous that she had communicated her anxiety to me. Madame Fournier led us directly to a room containing a table with a rubber cover. Then she excused herself for a moment.

Susan seized my arm and squeezed it hard. "I'm afraid," she whispered.

"Oh, for God's sake," I said, "calm down. She comes well recommended. People do this every day. It's really nothing." My heart was thumping and my mouth felt dry. I wanted to get out of there.

"Maybe I'm making a mistake," she said.

"Well, then, don't do it," I said. I spoke more loudly than I intended. She shrank away as if I had slapped her. "You've had plenty of time to think about it. You can't have it, you can't keep it, you don't want to give it away. So what's the alternative? Make a decision, and stick with it."

Her eyes filled with tears. "It's easy for you to talk," she said bitterly. "You're a man."

Madame Fournier returned with a pile of towels and a kettle. "Tout suite, mes enfants," she said.

Susan had given me the money ahead of time, so that I could play the husband. I counted it out into Madame's hand. She counted it over again and thanked me. I told her I had to go to work, and she said I should come back any time after noon. I kissed Susan on the cheek; it was ice cold. "Good luck," I said. "I'll see you later."

Elmer Long, my roommate from the hospital, was waiting for me in the office when I got there. He already smelled of alcohol, but he wanted to go out to a café. So we went to sit on the terrace of Le Select; this was the best entertainment Paris had to offer: just watching the world go by on the wide pavement of the Champs Élysée. Elmer said he wanted a fin with his coffee, but I insisted that he not have it. "You keep up that drinking and you'll have to go back to the hospital," I said. I believed he drank so much because he was lonely, and it was easy to talk to bartenders.

"Why don't you go home?" I asked.

He shook his white head. "I like it here. And I'm doin' God's will."

"What is His will?"

"What I'm doin'." I looked at him, and he added, "We're all part of the great plan."

After the garçon had brought the coffee I said, "You don't know God's plan and I don't know it. Nobody does."

"God is the great scientist," Elmer said. "He keeps improving man's character and intelligence. Every generation is a little better, and a little smarter."

"And a little more plentiful," I said. "The earth is going to be overpopulated in a hundred years. Is that part of the plan?"

"I don't know," Elmer said. "Nobody knows. But maybe he's going to send us out to populate other worlds."

That stopped me. "I've got to get back to work," I said. I stood up. "But before I go, I want you to promise me something."

"I know. You're just like the doctor. You want me to stop drinkin'."

"That's right. Can't you give up brandy? It'll kill you, you know that. I suppose wine or beer would be all right, if you have to have it, but you've got to give up the hard stuff. Your kidneys are bad. You're not as young as you were." I put some coins in my saucer. "See you later."

"The reason I came to see you," Elmer said, before I could walk away, "I was wonderin' if you could help me

latch onto a lady friend. I need some female companionship. I don't want a whore."

I thought of an American woman who hung out at the
Viking Bar. She seemed to be hard up and lonely. All I
knew was her first name, Bernice. I suggested that Elmer
meet me at the Viking after work. "But be sober," I said.

He promised he would.

In the afternoon I went back to the rue Bonaparte.
Susan was lying on the velour sofa, her face pale, her hair
disarranged. She smiled when she saw me and got up
slowly. Madame Fournier helped her with her coat and
she put her own hat on, at an odd angle. I moved auto-
matically to straighten it for her, and she caught at my
arm and closed her eyes. "Elle va bien?" I asked Madame.

"Oui, Monsieur, trés bien. Mais écoutez. Explique-lui
qu'il ne faut pas touche ce que j'ai mis dedans pour au
moins vingt-quatre heures. Comprendez-vous? Il faut
faire bien attention. C'est trés importante."

I said I understood, and we shook hands and left. I
had to help Susan down the few steps to the street and
when we got a cab she lay across the seat; I sat on the
jump seat.

"Listen," I said. "Madame said it was important. She—
there's something she put. . . Well, whatever it is, it's still
there, and you're not supposed to touch it for twenty-four
hours. It's supposed to stay there for twenty-four hours.
It's important."

She looked at me and began to laugh. Her laughter
had an edge of hysteria.

"Shh," I said. "You'll wake the dead."

It slipped out before I thought. She stopped laughing
abruptly. "What a terrible thing to say!" she said, and
burst into tears.

"I'm sorry," I said. I moved across and sat next to her, so that she could lean against me. "Please don't cry, Susan. It was terrible; I didn't think. Please don't cry." I gave her my handkerchief. "Was it very bad?" I asked.

"It was lousy," she said. She blew her nose.

"No anesthetic?"

"No. Nothing. I couldn't see what she was doing, but it hurt like hell. And it still hurts. Could you ask the driver to slow down? I really can't stand all this jolting."

I spoke to him, and we slowed down somewhat. I helped her into the lobby, when we got to her hotel. "Can you manage from here?" I asked.

"Oh, yes," she said. "I feel a little better." Her face was not quite as white as it had been in the cab, so I walked her to the elevator. Just before she entered it she kissed me on the cheek. "I can never thank you enough."

"I'm glad I was here to help," I said, embarrassed.

"I could never have done it without you," she said.

I couldn't help smiling. "And Walter," I said.

She smiled back. "Oh, you!" she said.

When she left Paris a few days later I took her to the station. "Be careful," I said in the cab, "when you get back to Walter. We don't want to have to go through this again."

"Oh, I'll never go through this again," she said. Her color was normal and her eyes were bright. She was an extraordinarily pretty girl. "From now on, to hell with men."

At the station we followed the porter into a second-class car. He stacked her luggage on a shelf and I insisted on giving him the tip.

"Too bad you have to go so soon," I said. "You haven't seen much of Paris."

"I haven't seen anything of it. And I've dreamed of coming here ever since I was a child. I haven't taken a ride on the Seine, I haven't gone to the Louvre, or Versailles, I haven't even been up in the Eiffel Tower."

"You've got to come back some time and I'll take you sight-seeing," I said. "And now that you've given up men, what are you going to do for amusement at home?"

She grimaced and pulled off her hat. "I'm thinking I'll become a nun and retire from the world."

"Well, don't do it until you see Walter first," I said.

She hesitated. "I don't know why I should tell you this," she said. "But I don't think the baby was Walter's. I think it might have been his son's." There was a long pause. I tried to think of something to say. Then a bell rang and someone shouted a warning. I bent to kiss her cheek. She followed me to the vestibule. As I got there, the train began to move. "Au 'voir," I said. "Give my love to my double-first cousin." I swung off just before the car cleared the shed. Then I stood and watched her wave a handkerchief until the train dwindled off down the track.

When I left the office that evening I went directly to the Viking to meet Elmer. He wasn't there, so I went ahead and ordered lamb stew and a beer. While I was eating, Bernice wandered in. I rose and called to her, and she came over to the table. She was small and pale, with dark hair and tired eyes. Her blue sheath dress had seen better days.

"Won't you join me for dinner?" I asked.

She eyed my stew. "I *am* hungry," she said. I pulled a chair out for her and she sat down. After I had given her order to the waiter, I said I was glad she had come by, because I had wanted to introduce her to someone. "How're you getting along?" I said.

She shrugged, and took a sip of my beer. "Oh, so so."

"Still posing at the Beaux Arts?"

"Now and then."

"I suppose it doesn't pay too well."

She shrugged again. "Ten francs an hour. Who is this you want me to meet? An artist?"

"Well, no. Actually, he's a preacher."

"Oh, my God!"

The waiter brought her stew with some rolls and a glass of wine. She began to eat ravenously.

"You're starved," I said. "I don't see why you stay here. You really ought to go home. Where are you from in the States?"

"Pennsylvania," she said. "Wilkes-Barre. I'd go back. But I don't have the money."

"Have you tried the American Aid Society? Maybe they'd help you get home."

She made a face. "They'd want me to pay 'em back. And I don't have anybody in Wilkes-Barre any more. I'd be no better off there than I am here. I've got nobody."

"How'd you get here anyway?"

"Worked my way over on a ship, and jumped it with a guy."

"Where's the guy now?"

She busily polished off the remains of the stew with a piece of roll. "I don't know."

"Well," I said, "this American I want you to meet is alone too. He really needs somebody."

At this point, as if on cue, Elmer came in. I was dismayed to see that he was drunk, despite my warning to him. He was too drunk to see us; I had to go over and get him and bring him to the table. I eased him into a chair and introduced him to Bernice, who was looking at him warily.

"Bring me a whiskey," he said to her.

"Elmer," I said. "This is the lady I told you about.

Remember? I wish you hadn't been drinking tonight. I asked you not to."

Elmer looked at me sadly. "Yes," he said, "I've made mistakes. I'm sorry, I apologize. But people shouldn't talk about me, people shouldn't turn against me. We all make mistakes. We're all victims. Don't talk against your fellow man." He looked at Bernice. "You shouldn't make that mistake," he said.

I signalled to Billie, the chubby British bartender, and asked him to bring Elmer some coffee.

"Whiskey," Elmer said.

"Damn it, Elmer," I said. "You can't have any whiskey. You've got to give it up. Are you stupid or what?" He looked at me sorrowfully. I was angry partly because I disliked the role he was forcing me to play. He was making me act like a guardian or a parent and he was a lot older than I was and he should have known more about life than I did. And he was a preacher, or he had been—a kind of teacher, a man of God. He should have gotten help from God, or from the Bible. I was an incongruous guru.

"You need something to eat," Bernice said.

When the waiter brought the coffee, I ordered some stew for Elmer. He drank a little of the coffee, but he obviously did not want any stew. He got up suddenly. I assumed he was going to the toilet, but then I noticed he was heading for the door. I suppose he was going someplace where he could get a drink, and where I was not going to be present to upset him. There was a commotion outside the door just as I reached it. Bernice was behind me. Elmer had apparently walked into some people who were trying to enter, and he had lost his balance. Two men were helping him get up.

"I'll take care of him," I said. He had apparently scraped his chin in the fall; it was bleeding.

"Don't let 'em talk about me," he said piteously to me.

I felt quite desperate. "Will you go home with him in a cab?" I asked Bernice. "Won't you just see that he gets to bed all right?"

She hesitated. I reached into his pocket and took out his wallet and handed it to her. "His wife died," I said. "He misses her."

"Oh, all right," she said. "What the hell."

I herded them into a cab. "Take care of him," I said. I watched them drive off and, with a sigh of relief, went back into the Viking to pay the bill.

A couple of nights later I was in the Viking bar with a Texan and his Australian girl friend when Bernice and Elmer came in together. I invited them to have dinner with us. Elmer was looking rather pale and was unusually quiet. But we were all unusually quiet because Jack Hough, the Texan, dominated the evening, with remarks like: "Can I write? Why, don't make me laugh! I'm the best damn writer this side of Timbuktu!" The Australian girl informed us that she was half-Tahitian, could drink any man under the table and was the best bed partner in France, if not the world.

At points in the evening, while Elmer went off to the toilet, and Jack was turning his attention occasionally to the Australian, I asked Bernice how things were going with her and Elmer. She said she had put him to bed that first evening with soothing comments; he had been very upset about his life. She had had to promise him she would come back to breakfast the next morning, and he had told her to take a hundred francs. She had taken five hundred, had come back for breakfast: they had eaten at the Dôme and she had talked him out of having an eye-opener, and then had stayed with him all day to keep him from drinking.

"I don't know," she said thoughtfully. "He's pretty old and crazy. But what the hell. You know, he might straighten out. Wouldn't that be something?"

When dinner was finished the three of us parted company with Jack and his friend. I went home to soothing silence, and Bernice went home with Elmer.

XI
A Visit from Hearst

Alan Finn, who had been unceremoniously demoted from city editor to copy editor, had worked on the *Herald* for years, and knew the French—their culture, character and government—better than any American I knew. He was a good newspaperman. Physically he was unprepossessing, having a heavily scarred face and a large aquiline nose. He had never married, but he was living happily with Enriqueta Sorenson, a stunningly beautiful woman who had been born in Spain of a Spanish mother and a Swedish father. She had her mother's brown eyes and olive skin, and her father's blonde hair. She wore brightly-colored clothes, and her long fingers were adorned with blood-red nails. It was impossible for almost any man to be in a room with her and be unaware of her. She and Alan were a rather incongruous couple.

They did not spend as much time in cafés as the rest of us. Now and then I would see them at the Dôme, Lipp's or Deux Magots and I always enjoyed their company. Enriqueta's English was not good, and neither was her

French, but she had a radiant smile and a musical laugh, and Alan was always interesting.

One evening I was in Lipp's with a visiting fireman named Archer Jones, a tall, handsome Virginian about my age who had arrived in Paris the day before. I don't recall who told him to look me up, but I think it was one of my Atlanta friends who had known him at the University of Virginia. The Jones family business printed offering envelopes for churches. It had been a profitable business, handed down through three generations of Joneses, but Archer's father had committed suicide, and the business had recently been sold to settle the estate. Archer had been glad when it was sold, because he had been working there, and he hated it; he said the place reminded him of a mortuary. He had an income from a small trust and he could do pretty much what he pleased. Like a good many of us, he had come to Paris because he wanted to be a writer.

Allan and Enriqueta came in to Lipp's while we were there, and I introduced Archer to them. We shared a table because the place was full. Lipp's was popular with French politicians who enjoyed its delicious German beer. Because of its large French clientele, Lipp's only tolerated foreigners; the management demanded propriety from its guests. Consequently every American newsman had been booted out of the place at one time or another for loud or profane behavior.

Allen and I began to talk about the current turmoil in Spain; Enriqueta, who had been born in Malaga, was particularly interested in the conversation. Then Allen, lowering his voice, got onto the subject of the French war debt. He said that the French newspapers, regardless of their political coloration, gave their readers the impression that the money which President Hoover was trying to collect from the French government was payment for supplies left in France by the Americans after the war, rather than what it really was: money lent to France during the war.

There was a certain amount of tension in American-French relations then. William Randolph Hearst had just been in Paris with Marion Davies and an entourage of friends, staying at the Crillon. I had met them when I was in Hollywood because of my friendship with Miss Davies' niece, Pepé Lederer. So I was assigned to interview Hearst, and was in the Hearst suite when a French official arrived and announced that Hearst was persona non grata in France, and would have to leave the country within four days. The official reason given was that Hearst had bought and published secret documents relating to Anglo-French naval negotiations. But I think another more damaging reason for his expulsion was an interview Hearst had given the *Frankfurter Zeitung* a few days earlier, when he had been in Bad Nauheim taking the baths. He had assailed the Versailles Treaty and what he called French "domination" of Germany. The interview had been given wide publicity, and the French were angry about it.

Hearst did not appear to be angry when he was given this expulsion order. Instead he made a little speech to Miss Davies, Harry Crocker, a flunky of his who was present, and me. He said in all his sixty-seven years he had never been so gratified. He considered the expulsion order recognition that he had done well the job in journalism which he had been doing for nearly fifty years. "I have kept the people of my country informed," he said, "and by doing so I have offended a great nation."

Actually, we could all tell that he was furious. He added, in a voice which he was controlling with difficulty, that he had no intention of remaining for four days in a country that did not want him. And so without unpacking at all he and his party left at once for London, where he wrote a manifesto which appeared on the front pages of all of his newspapers and many other papers as well, including the *Herald:*

> I have no complaint to make. The French officials were extremely polite. They said I was an enemy of France, and a danger in their midst. They made me feel quite important. They said I could stay in France a little while longer if I desired and they would take a chance on nothing disastrous happening to the Republic.
>
> But I told them I did not want to take the responsibility of endangering the great French nation, that America had saved it once during the war and I would save it again by leaving it. . .
>
> The reason for the strained relations—to use the proper diplomatic term—was the publication of the secret Anglo-French Treaty two years ago by the Hearst papers, which upset some international apple carts, but informed the American people.
>
> I think, however, that the general attitude of the French press toward our opposing the United States entrance into the League of Nations, or any protective pact to involve our country in the quarrels of European powers, is mainly responsible. Also there might have been some slight irritation at the occasional intimations in our papers that France, now being the richest nation in the world, might use some of the German indemnity to pay her honest debts to America, especially because if it had not been for America she would now be paying indemnity instead of receiving it.
>
> But being a competent journalist and a loyal

American makes a man persona non grata in France. I think I can endure the situation without loss of sleep.

We discussed this event at Lipp's that evening. I said I couldn't help being a little pleased about Hearst's obvious discomfiture, since I had once worked for him and did not admire his brand of journalism. But we all agreed that the French had really behaved foolishly by taking such drastic action against him. I thought he had had the last word when he said to us in the Crillon that France was like the effeminate youth who went to call on his best girl. Entering the parlor and finding her in the arms of another, the young man retreated into the hall, took his rival's umbrella, and broke it over his knee, saying, "There! I hope it rains!"

We were all amused at this—except Archer. He did not appear to be paying any attention to the conversation; he was staring fixedly at Enriqueta. When he and I left to do some bistro-crawling, he said, "She's gorgeous! Are they married?"

I explained their relationship and added, "And he's my friend. Don't forget the Lord's commandment: Thou shalt not covet thy neighbor's wife."

"Well, but she's not his wife. Anyway, she's a real beauty."

We ended our evening at the Dôme, and a day or so later I left Paris for a two-week vacation in Nice. I was the guest of a writer named Tod Robins, who was the author of several pot-boilers, one of which, *The Unholy Three*, had been made into a movie. He had a nice house, a car and a chauffeur. His house was on a hillside overlooking Villefranche; just below it, on the seashore, was Somerset Maugham's magnificent villa, which had its own small

sandy beach, one of the few in the area. Tod took me to
Maugham's beach for a swim. Then we went to the villa
for lunch. Among the guests was H.G. Wells. Maugham
had thirteen servants, of which seven were gardeners. I
was overawed. It was like visiting royalty.

I wrote Mother about it:

> A number of famous writers live along the
> Riviera: Wells in Grasse, Frank Harris in Nice, James
> Barrie and Michael Arlen in Cannes. I have come to
> the conclusion that the soil here is rich for story-
> flowering; I told Tod I yearned to own a piece of
> ground.
>
> The next day he took me to Eze, a spectacular
> cluster of houses on the high cliffs between Nice and
> Monte Carlo. We found a tiny lot for sale there; it ad-
> joined a villa owned by the king of Sweden. The price
> was forty thousand francs—one thousand, six hun-
> dred dollars—so I made a down-payment on it of one
> thousand francs. It's not much, but it gives me a toe
> in the door.
>
> The house I envison will cost, I'm told, around
> three thousand dollars. It will be made of stone, and
> have one large room with a beamed ceiling, a fire-
> place, of course, and windows overlooking the sea.
> The bedroom and bath will have a balcony, and there
> will be a small dining area and kitchen. I'm ablaze
> with excitement, although I don't know when I'll get
> the money to finish paying for the land, let alone
> build the house.

XII
Domestic Relations

The evening I returned to Paris I went by the Dôme on my way home. Allen was sitting on the terrace alone, with a snifter of brandy in front of him. I knew he ordinarily drank only beer. I went up and pulled out a chair at his table.

"Hi," he said without warmth. "I see you're back."

"Where's Enriqueta?"

He looked away. "God knows."

"What do you mean?"

"I mean I don't know. I mean she's gone."

The waiter came up. I ordered a beer and he ordered another brandy. Two Frenchmen came and sat near us. Both had moustaches and pot bellies; they were wearing those awful black suits businessmen wore.

"This friend of yours," Allen said. "Name of Jones. Where'd you find him?" Everything was quite clear to me. "I didn't find him," I said defensively. "He found me. Friend of a friend, visiting. I really don't know him from Adam."

"It's been going on ever since you introduced them, I guess. When I got home yesterday, she was gone. No note, nothing. That's almost the worst part. She should have talked to me about it."

The waiter brought the drinks.

"If she'd come to me and said, 'Allen, I've fallen in love with someone else' or anything. If she'd at least told me why she wanted to leave."

I was angry with Archer, and I took it out on Allen. "What the hell difference would that make?" I said. "What difference would it make whether she told you or not?"

"She might have been friendly about it. She might have been grateful. After all, I picked her up from the gutter." His eyes were filled with tears of self-pity. "I don't blame Jones. I don't blame either of them. It's nobody's fault, really. These things happen. But I do think she might have talked it over with me; she might have given me some thanks for what I've done for her."

I couldn't stand listening to it. "I've got to go home to bed," I said. "Listen, it's not the end of the world. You'll find someone else."

He hardly seemed to notice when I left.

Most Americans in Paris lived on the left bank and went to the same bistros there. In order to avoid running into Allen, Archer rented an apartment near the Place du Tertre, the square up on the hill in Montmartre, behind the Sacré Coeur. He and Enriqueta did not come to the Left Bank at all. But one day on my way back to the office on the Champs Élysée I saw them sitting on the terrace of the Select. Archer called to me and I went over to them reluctantly. I shook hands with Archer, although I didn't want to.

"How was your trip?" he asked.

"I had a better time than Allen is having," I said. I was pretty angry.

"It's your fault," Archer said coyly, "You introduced us."

"Allen Finn will never forgive me," I said. "I've probably lost a friend. What a lousy trick you played on him, both of you."

"I never love Allen," Enriqueta said. "He good to me. I no want hurt him." She knew that I knew she had been a dancer—maybe even a prostitute—when Allen had met her; she had been broke and hungry in Malaga.

"It was just one of those things," Archer said. "I saw her and she saw me and that's all there was to it. We didn't want to hurt anybody."

"We're in love," Enriqueta said.

"Well, it isn't really any of my business," I said. I was stll angry. "I'm going to be late for work. So long. Good luck."

A week or so later I received a pneumatique from Archer. He wanted to see me, but of course he couldn't come to the *Herald* offices for fear of seeing Allen. I sent a message back asking him to come up to my place the next morning.

I could not behave naturally with him. I knew I was being stiff, but he relaxed in my big chair without appearing to notice.

"I need a little help from you on the problem I'm having," he said. "I've got to go home. Something has come up about my father's estate."

I waited. "What's the problem?"

"Well, there's Enriqueta. I can't take her with me, you know that. My mother would have a fit. And I don't want to just walk out on her. Would you consider taking her in? She doesn't know anything about this."

I was shocked. "Do you intend to come back?"

"Well, I hope so. But I can't leave her any money—my income's only two hundred a month and I don't know what the future holds. I don't want to go off and just leave her in the lurch."

"Listen," I said. "I think Enriqueta's a knockout. Everybody does. But she can't stay here. Allen Finn is my friend, remember?"

"Do you think he might take her back?" he asked calmly. "I've got to leave Friday, I'm in kind of a hurry. Would you ask him?"

"He'll probably feel like killing you."

"Then don't ask him until I'm gone."

"Well, look, I can ask him. But you've got to under-stand that you can't come back again if he agrees. I mean, you'll have to find yourself another girl."

"I understand that," he said. He paused and looked thoughtful. "It's really too bad I can't stick around a while. She and I have a good thing going." He got up. "Well, I can't tell you how much I appreciate your help here. It's a great relief."

"But you can't be sure Allen will do it," I said, rising too. "What if he doesn't? He's been hit pretty hard, you know."

"Oh, she'll be all right," he said easily. "She'll find someone. She's too good-looking to be alone for long."

"She was in a mess when Allen met her," I said grimly.

"She'll land on her feet," he said. "And listen, thanks again. Be seeing you."

When I got to the office I asked Allen to come into a conference room with me.

"Sit down," I said. "I've got something to tell you. I

hope you'll think it's good news." He sat down tentatively and looked at me. I felt rather nervous. "Enriqueta wants to come back to you," I said.

He looked at me. "You're joking," he said.

"Would I joke about a thing like this?" I asked indignantly. "I know how you feel about it. I'm telling you Enriqueta knows she made a mistake; she wants to come back."

He sat silent for a moment. "What about the guy?" he said finally. "How does he feel about this?"

"Well, actually," I said, "he's gone. He went back to Virginia."

He raised his brows. "He's left her?"

"Well, he might come back. But she doesn't care. She's through with him."

"The son-of-a-bitch," Allen said. He sat brooding for a while. "She's decided to come back because she needs a meal ticket," he said.

"I know it looks that way," I said. "But he left her money. And he said he would come back. He had to go home because of his father's estate. I know that's true, because he told me about the estate when I first met him."

"Enriqueta sent you here?"

"She sure did," I said, lying my head off. "She was afraid to approach you herself. Believe me, Allen, she's learned her lesson. She'll never do anything like this again."

He got up. "I have to think about it," he said.

"You don't want to hold a grudge," I said. "Forgive and forget. Everybody makes mistakes, Allen."

"She put me through hell," he said. "I have to think about it."

He walked slowly out of the room. I went out to the nearest post office and sent Enriqueta a pneumatique asking her to meet me that night at the Deux Magots.

She met me there about nine o'clock and we went across the street to Lipp's for dinner. I ordered knockwurst, sauerkraut and a beer. She wasn't hungry and settled for a brandy.

"Well," I said, "he's gone now. You're alone. Now what are you going to do?"

She shrugged. "I wait for him," she said.

"But supposing he doesn't come back?"

She looked into my eyes. "He will come back," she said.

"But what if he doesn't? I'll tell you frankly that I got the distinct impression from him that he might not come back."

"But he tell me," she said.

"And you believe him," I said. "Did he leave you any money?"

"A little."

"Enough for you to eat and pay the rent? For how long?"

She shrugged again.

"Well, you've got to think of the future. You have to move, anyway."

She nodded. The waiter brought the order, and I waited until he left.

"Listen, Enriqueta," I said. "Now, don't get mad if I say this. I really think you ought to go back to Allen."

She put down her brandy glass, and looked surprised. "But he would not," she said. "He would never."

"I think he will. I spoke to him. I told him Archer had left. And I'm telling you, Enriqueta, I think he still loves you. I mean, he was furious at Archer for going off and leaving you. He's worried about you."

She looked doubtful.

"You care for him a little, don't you?" I asked.

"He fine man," she said. "Very good to me. I like him. But Archer, he comes back."

"No, no, he won't. He's no good, Enriqueta. You should forget about him. Why, do you know what he suggested?" She looked interested. "He suggested that you move in with *me*. Of course that's out of the question," I added hastily, "and I know you feel the same way. Allen is a friend of mine. But it shows you how low this guy is. And he's fickle—you know, you can't depend on him. But you know you can depend on Allen Finn."

As I was speaking I saw Allen enter the restaurant; Enriqueta's back was to the room. "He's here now," I said.

She turned quickly and looked, and then turned back to me.

"Poor Allen," she said. Her full lips trembled.

Allen did not see us. He had joined Charles Braydon, an elderly Englishman who wrote mysteries, at Braydon's regular table. The writer was a fixture at Lipp's.

"Why don't I ask him to come over?" I said. "It's a great opportunity."

I had finished most of my knockwurst anyway. I went over to Braydon's table, and after the usual courtesies, I told Allen Enriqueta was at my table, and she wished to speak with him.

"I hear her new boyfriend has flown the coop," Charles said. He was drunk.

Allen flushed red and then turned white. He got up and followed me through the crowded room. He was carrying his umbrella and his black homburg. Enriqueta looked up at him and wiped a tear from her eye with one slim finger with its long lacquered fingernail.

"Hello, Allen," she said.

Staring at her fixedly, Allen sank into my chair.

"I see some friends," I said. "I'll see you later." I picked up my wine glass and went back to join Charles.

When I left the restaurant a considerable time later, Allen and Enriqueta were still sitting at the table, talking.

Archer Jones did not return to Paris while I was there. Years later when I was living in California, in Laguna Beach, I met him again. He was still trying to get published; he was married to a beautiful woman. He had drained his trust fund and I was able to help him a little financially; he never repaid these small loans. A few years later I heard that he had been sued for debts and had turned up in the local courthouse. Soon after that he left his wife and wandered off. The last time I heard about him he was apparently living on Skid Row in Los Angeles.

Allen and Enriqueta were living together in apparent harmony when I left Paris. She was working as a model for couturiers.

XIII
Henry Ford in Cherbourg and a Sad Loss

I wrote to Mother:

My project of a dream house on the Riviera has fallen through. Lacy Kastner offered to lend me enough money to buy the land, but I couldn't talk a banker into lending me enough money to build the house. I have no collateral, apparently. My modest wage is barely sufficient to keep me alive and the banker was not interested in my forthcoming novel. He said he was sorry, but he didn't look sorry. I guess I'd better wait until I garner a backlog of cash before I try to become a landowner.

The proofs of *Gun Girl* came last week, and I've been busy proofreading them. This is Sunday, and I have to get them on the *Aquitania* Wednesday. McBride plans to publish in January. Too bad it couldn't appear before Christmas. I suppose it's hard for a writer to judge his own work, and the story may really be engrossing, but now, reading it for the umpteenth time, I find it awfully shallow. I'm about to finish *Men Are April When They Woo*. It's pretty long—about 140,000 words. I've rewritten it many times and I don't dare read it again from start to finish for fear it's no good. I hope to get it to the publisher by the time *Gun Girl* comes out. It'll be a relief to get rid of it, and I hope McBride gives me a larger advance this time.

I'm becoming disenchanted with newspaper work, and I'd like to move on to something else. Day to day reporting can be pretty dull. There are times of course when it is lots of fun. What happens to people on the staff here is often more interesting than the news we write. For example, last week I went with George Rehm and Waldo Pierce to George's hideaway in the Valley of the Chevreuse. We had a fine time lapping up the local oh-be-joyful and were sleeping so soundly the other morning that we weren't disturbed when a cow wandered into the two-room house which has dirt floors and no doors. We were surprised to see her when we woke up, and we promptly milked her and drank the result for breakfast. Waldo is painting a picture of the scene, but he's changing the cow to an enraged bull. Obviously more dramatic impact.

George Rehm is one of the nicest, most gentle and likeable men I've ever met. He spends a lot of his time listening to other people's troubles, giving them sympathy and advice when he can. He drinks with them, worries with them and cheers them up. He writes very well, but he is a procrastinator and he may never write that great American novel because he spends so much time helping other people. His son is a really impressive child—very smart and personable. He is walking now and always looking for chairs to climb on.

Last night I stopped at the Dôme before I came home and had a drink with John Holland, a notable

Canadian painter; Joe (the Bum) Ludovic, a Polish sculptor, and Otto Schmit, an American artist who has lived here since the war. Holland said that he was giving up painting; he had won all the prizes an artist could want, but had made very little money. He said he wanted to go back to Canada and grow tobacco. Otto told him not to be foolish.

"If you keep on painting," Otto said, "you'll be famous like Whistler."

"Sure," Holland said. "After I'm dead. I won't give a damn then."

"Art is something you do because you have to," Joe the Bum said. "It hasn't got anything to do with money. It always surprises me when people buy the damn stuff."

Otto and Holland began to reminisce about the good old days before the war. Holland said that Whistler was a good artist "despite the bloody critics." Otto said that there had been two billiard tables in the Dôme—in the back room, where Whistler, Booth Tarkington, Jack London, and other famous people had played poker. He said the game never stopped. It's hard to believe that went on in the Dôme, which is now one of the busiest cafés in the city, crowded night and day.

Eric Hawkins assigned me to meet Henry Ford who was coming to Europe for the first time since his Peace Ship visit in 1915. He was scheduled to arrive in Cherbourg on the *Europa*, a German liner, due to dock about five o'clock the next morning. "He's tough on newspapermen," Eric said, "so be prepared." I went to the *Herald* morgue and got the Ford file. It was huge. I took all the clippings with me to study on the train.

Ford was then sixty-eight. He was one of the most famous men in the world: in 1914 he had established an eight-hour work day and more than doubled the prevailing laboring wage to five dollars a day. In that same year he had launched the first large-scale assembly line. And of course his sales of automobiles had revolutionized America.

In 1915 he had decided that he was a sage and a prophet and that God had chosen him to put a stop to the war and its "silly killings". He thought that with his money and his power he could put an end to war forever. He vowed publicly that he would get the boys out of the trenches by Christmas. His plan was based on "The Neutral Conference of Continuous Meditation" devised by a Hungarian woman named Rosika Schwimmer. He chartered a large Scandinavian-American Line Ship, the *Oscar II* and invited many famous people to go along with him. He was turned down by John Wanamaker, who called the enterprise "a mission of generous heart, fat pocketbook, but no plan", and Theodore Roosevelt, who had won a Nobel Peace Prize, and called the venture "ridiculous". William Howard Taft, another invited guest, reportedly laughed so hard at the idea that he shook up the 23rd Street Ferry.

But others accepted. Rosika Schwimmer was one, of course. Another was Ada Morse Clark, secretary to the chancellor of Stanford University. Mrs Clark did not arrive in New York from California until December 3rd, the day before the Peace Ship was scheduled to sail. She had no passport. She located a photographer in New York who took her picture by flashlight at 11 p.m. Then she took the 12:30 train to Washington. She arrived at the State Department building at seven in the morning, and persuaded a night watchman to let her in. From there she telephoned the chief of the Passport Division, convinced his butler to awaken him, and talked the chief into coming to the office immediately. She sent a taxi for him. The taxi got lost, and the chief finally arrived at his office in a vegetable truck. Mrs Clark obtained her passport and arrived in New York an hour before sailing time, tired but happy.

Another celebrity invited to join Ford was Dr Charles Giffin Pease, the head of the Anti-Smoking League. Dr Pease had gained fame by riding streetcars and snatching cigarettes from the lips and fingers of his fellow passengers. Since Ford also hated smoking, Dr Pease was on his list of favored guests. He did actually show up, but unfortunately he was booked to travel in the same cabin with a woman named Annette Hazelton. Ford found out about it, and went into a rage, called Pease an immoral fellow and demanded that he vacate the ship.

"There's nothing immoral about it," Pease said. "She's my secretary."

But Ford was adamant, so the ship sailed without Dr Pease. But on the ship were Judge Ben Lindsey of Denver, who believed in trial marriage, and clergymen, politicians, educators, businessmen and students. There were four children on board, thirty-four journalists, three newsreel cameramen and two stowaways, one of whom was a Danish lad who said he just wanted to go home for Christmas.

I read all about this on my way to Cherbourg, where I arrived late in the evening. I decided not to register in a hotel. I was afraid I would oversleep and miss everything. So I stayed in a café until it closed at midnight and then went to the dock, where I was told the ship's tender would come in, and fell asleep on a bench. Despite all these precautions, I managed to oversleep anyway. When I woke, the tender had left the dock to pick up the passengers from the *Europa*.

I stood in a funk of disappointment, watching the

Henry Ford

tender pull away. But then I saw a white launch detach itself from the *Europa* and head toward me. "That would be Mr Ford," I said to myself. And it was. The launch came directly to where I was standing and Ford and his wife and some friends stepped off. There was no mistaking him; for years his picture had appeared in newspapers and magazines, and there he was: tall and skinny in a gray suit and a gray felt hat. I felt awed.

I fell into step beside him, and introduced myself. Some of the men with him, who looked like bodyguards, glared at me, but Ford kept his eyes straight in front of him and did not give me so much as a glance.

"I talk to newspaper reporters by appointment only," he said coldly.

"I beg your pardon, sir." I kept pace with him. "I've been here all night. I've come all the way from Paris. The world wants to know why you are here."

He did not break his stride. "I was misquoted in New York," he said. "How do I know you won't misquote me?"

"You don't, and you'll never find out if you don't give me a chance."

"Well, I'm not going to give you a chance."

He got into one of two Lincolns which had been ordered to drive him and his party to Paris.

"But Mr Ford," I said, leaning into the car window, "at least tell me where you are going."

"You'll find out," he said. Then he said, "Drive on," to the chauffeur and wound up the window in my face. The car pulled away, leaving me boiling in its dust.

On the train back to Paris I wrote a story about exactly what had happened, quoting the old bastard word for word. I wanted the public to know what a heartless curmudgeon the famous man was.

But when I handed it in, the managing editor killed

the story. "There's no news in it," he said. "And besides he may be able to sue us for libel somehow."

Ford finally consented to a press conference in Paris. All the local correspondents and reporters were invited, including me. It took place in the Plaza-Athenée Hotel. Mr Ford sat on a divan with his arms folded. He didn't answer questions; rather, he lectured and pontificated. His pet theory at the time was that people should work six months a year in factories, and six months on farms. He expounded on this at length. We all had the impression that he had no patience with people who disagreed with him.

Henry Wales, the correspondent for the *Chicago Tribune*, tried to change the subject by giving the manufacturer a compliment on his product. "I drove Model T ambulances during the war," Henry said, "and they were absolutely marvelous. We drove them up to the front lines through muck and mire and they brought us and the wounded safely back. You would have been proud of them."

Ford scowled. "I don't want my cars used like that. I don't believe in war."

He was so rude that we were all embarrassed. If anyone had told me then that one day I would become a public relations man for Ford, I would have suggested he change his brand of opium. But I did become one. I was hired by Ford at the beginning of the second World War, when Ford was turning out war machines, including B-24s. When I joined it, the company was financially shaky and the war may well have saved it from going under. When I was alone with him once in Dearborn, Michigan, I mentioned the Cherbourg encounter to him but he said he did not remember it.

Ford was an almost unbelievable character, a kind of

idiot-genius, without a sense of humor and without much empathy, and with a one-track mind. He seemed almost to have come from another planet, but he caused a social revolution, the effects of which go on today. He was not well-educated, but he did have some admirable innovative ideas. He had some zany ones too. He believed that most medical illnesses came from eating refined sugar: he thought the sugar crystals would not dissolve, and damaged the membranes of the body.

In his personal relationships he appeared to be about as warm and friendly as a process server. I used to wonder how his wife could stand him.

XIV
An Evening on the Town with Sinclair Lewis

A couple of evenings after my encounter with Ford, Sinclair Lewis invited Elliot Paul and me to join him on a spree through the hooch houses. I was happy to go with him, hoping that some of his talent would rub off on me. At that time he was the most successful American writer. *Main Street,* published in 1920 and considered a major work of social satire, had been followed by *Babbitt* in 1922, *Arrowsmith* in 1925, *Elmer Gantry* in 1927, and *Dodsworth* in 1929. Finally in 1931, the year before our meeting, he had received the Nobel Prize for Literature.

We started at the Ritz Bar, which was for men only. It was one of the most famous saloons in the world, like the old Knickerbocker in New York, and the Raffles in Singapore. An oblong room, with mahogany furniture, it was more expensive than other Parisian bars and claimed a distinguished and affluent clientele. Frank Meyer, the bartender, was courted by maharajahs, nawabs, archdukes, sheiks and other potentates, as well as by the rich and famous. On the other side of Peacock Alley was a bar for women and their escorts, called, for some reason, the Black Hole of Calcutta. It was headquarters for a legendary group called "The Alimony Sisterhood": in those days Paris was the fashionable place to get a divorce. Members of the Sisterhood gathered in the Black Hole to gossip about husbands, past and present, and compare lawyers' fees.

By the time we had our second drink Lewis's personality had begun to percolate. Liquor brought out the best and the worst in him. Tall and skinny, he was anything but handsome, his hair sparse and colorless, his thin-jawed face mottled with acne. But he could be most amusing; he was something of an exhibitionist and he loved to perform. He became very lively at the Ritz and was even livelier by the time we moved to Henry's, our second stop. I noted down this limerick which he had composed himself and which he recited to a lady he had never seen before:

> There was a young lady of Real
> Who said, 'Dear, I don't like to cavil
> But honestly, dear,
> It goes better in here.
> You've confused something else with my navel.

Neither the lady nor her escort were amused. To disperse the chill, and to distract him, I asked Lewis about his writing habits. We were still fairly sober, and he always liked to help aspiring writers, so he told me his routine. He said he worked about seven hours a day, starting in the early morning but sometimes when the work was going well he would work all night.

"Good writing," he said, "depends on the seat of the pants. But the hardest part is rewriting. The first time you

Elliot Paul

write a story it can be fun, but as you edit and rewrite, it becomes more and more boring. After you've rewritten it four or five times you tend to lose faith in it, and by the time you've rewritten for the fourteenth or fifteenth time you become certain no one will ever read the damn thing."

Elliot agreed. He said that he had become so discouraged with a book he was writing recently that he had thrown the entire 50,000 word manuscript out the window and into the Seine. "I stood and watched the sheets float down the river," he said.

"Maybe the fish enjoyed them," Lewis said.

"No," Elliot said. "They were written in English. Seine fish read only French."

Lewis said that Hemingway had rewritten the ending of *A Farewell to Arms* more than sixty times; he said the only writer he knew of who could revise only once or twice and turn out a publishable piece was George Bernard Shaw. "Of course," he said, "what he writes is pretty awful. But even for him, that's not much editing."

Lewis said he was in the "digestive" stage now of a novel about a union leader. I suggested the Ford Motor Company as a good setting for a novel like that. Lewis agreed; he thought Ford would make a fine villain. But as for automobile manufacturers he had already written a novel about one. "That's *Dodsworth*," he said.

From Henry's we went on to Ciro's on the rue Danou, called the most American street in Paris. Ciro's had been funded by James Gordon Bennett, and *Herald* employees were always welcome there. The chausseur recognized Elliot and me, and we introduced Red Lewis. The chausseur had obviously never heard of him; he was polite but not fawning. I thought to myself, "This ignorant bastard doesn't know greatness when he sees it." I was definitely feeling the effects of the evening.

While we were at the bar, lapping up the juice, we told Red Ciro's story. Ciro was a small-boned Egyptian who had been born in Italy. James Gordon Bennett had met him when Ciro was headwaiter of a favorite restaurant of Bennett's in Monte Carlo. Bennett grew fond of Ciro and insisted that he wait on him whenever he came in for lunch. Since Bennett tipped lavishly, Ciro was able in time to save up enough money to buy a restaurant of his own. With Bennett's approval he rented the place next door and Bennett and his friends moved their custom there, effectively wrecking the original restaurant. When Bennett said he liked eating outdoors so that he could watch the passersby, Ciro put some tables on the sidewalk.

One day while Bennett was lunching, a policeman came up and told Ciro that it was against the law to put tables on the sidewalk, and they would have to be removed. Bennett lost his temper and hit the policeman with a plate, threatening to have him fired. "The Prince of Monaco is a friend of mine!" he shouted. "I'm coming back tomorrow. I want to sit at a table on this sidewalk, and I don't want anyone in this principality to try and stop me!" When he returned the next day all of the sidewalk tables were gone. Ciro was upset; he could not defy the police and he was afraid he was going to lose his best customer. He told Bennett it was all the fault of the restaurant next door. "They don't like the competition," he said. "It was they who called the police." Bennett said characteristically, "Let's buy the goddam place!" And he did. The two places were merged, and the city fathers allowed tables to be placed on the sidewalk. There the Commodore ate his lunches. Subsequently Ciro sold out and opened the place in Paris. Bennett and his friends made it an instant success.

One of the men at the bar that evening was Florence O'Neil, erstwhile European correspondent for a Pittsburg newspaper founded by his father. When his father died, leaving him a considerable sum of money, he became an outré barfly, a fixture at Ciro's and a bit of a nuisance. He shook Lewis's hand and said, "I'm glad to meet the great Sinclair Lewis. Have you heard the latest about Peggy Joyce? She's going to marry the Aga Khan." Then without a pause he launched into a vulgar story he said Buster Keaton had told him. It wasn't funny, but we laughed politely. Then he told another one that he said he had heard from Elsa Maxwell. That one wasn't funny either. He was about to tell one that Harry Lehr had told him when Lewis interrupted.

"We don't care who told you the story," he said. "Just be sure it's funny." Then Lewis told the old story about the piccolo player: the stage manager comes out and says, "Who called our piccolo player a son-of-a-bitch?" And the bum in the balcony yells, "Who called that son-of-a-bitch a piccolo player?" We had all heard the story before, but Lewis made it hilarious. Then he said to O'Neil, "Don't tell anyone I told you that story."

"I won't," O'Neil said. "I think I heard it first from the Dolly Sisters."

From Ciro's we went to the Bal St Severin, a low-class dance hall on the Left Bank, in Elliot's neighborhood. We stood at the bar and watched the dancers. The men, wearing corduroy trousers, neckerchiefs and berets, swung the girls, who wore short, split skirts and sweater shirts, in an Apache dance. Then a young girl with black hair sang "Parlez-moi d'Amour" in imitation of Lucienne Boyer, while a three-piece orchestra played her accompaniment. After a while Lewis became restless; he wanted to go to the Closerie des Lilas.

Sinclair Lewis

So thither we went and there between drinks we re-hashed George du Maurier's novel *Trilby,* some of which was set in the Closerie. I mentioned The Sphinx to Lewis and he said he wanted to see it. He said he had always been interested in bordellos but he had never been in one. "Since the beginning of time," Lewis said, "the only thing a female has had to help her is her body. So they gussie themselves up with make-up and do-dads, to at-tract the male. But being bounced by one man after an-other has got to be exhausting, monotonous and demean-ing. I would think it was a disheartening life."

When we got to The Sphynx we were all well-oiled. Elliot and I had switched to beer at the dance hall, but Lewis had stayed with the hard stuff and his personality had changed. A metamorphosis was taking place. My re-spect for him had verged on awe, so I could hardly be-lieve it when he became rambunctious at the bar, com-plaining that the drinks were too small and too expensive. He got into an argument with the bartender and the ruck-us grew so bad that a big bouncer came up and asked us to leave. When we finally managed to drag Lewis, still fuming, outside, Elliot decided he had had enough and bade us good-night.

I wanted to go home too, but Lewis was still angry and upset, and he said he needed another drink. I was afraid that he might get into more trouble, so I took him to the Viking. By the time we wobbled in there—two o'clock in the morning—he had calmed down. The place was crowded, but we found two seats at the bar. Lewis sat next to an attractive young woman with tanned skin and a long coal-black braid hanging down her back. She was drinking oxygenée in a long-stemmed glass and he asked her what it was. "It looks like soapy water," he said. Her name, she told him, was Nicole and she came from Tahiti.

Lewis turned to me and said in a sonorous voice, "I have here a Tahitian princess who drinks oxygen and gin and is looking for a husband to help her rule her island. Are you available?" I said I was. He turned back to her and said, "My friend here wants to marry you."

"I'll have to ask my husband," she said.

"Oh, so you've got a prince? A Tahitian?"

"No, he's from California." She slid off her stool. "That reminds me. I'd better go phone him."

"If you get him at this hour you'll win the telephone medal of honor. You'll probably get the President's palace."

"He'll do," she said. She drained her glass and left us. We didn't see her again.

Lewis began singing a song about tickling his grandfather's private parts with a feather. The other people at the bar thought it was funny, and encouraged him. Then he sang,

> Oh, the Dutch Company is the best company
> That ever came over from old Germany.,
> There's the Amsterdam Dutch and the Rotterdam
>   Dutch,
>
> And the Potsdam Dutch and the Goddam Dutch. . .

He basked in the general merriment, and was obviously having a good time. A young man asked if he knew the Christ cheerleader song:

> The game was played on Sunday
> In St Peter's back yard.
> Jesus he played fullback and
> Moses, he played guard.
> The angels on the sideline,

Christ, how they did yell! when
Jesus made that touchdown
Against the team from Hell.
Hold 'em Christ. . .

Lewis asked the young man to sing the song again so he could memorize it. Some of the other drunks gathered around Lewis, and they sang "Down By the Old Mill Stream," "Sweet Adeline," and a lot of other old tunes, including "The Cows in the Meadow Go Moo, Moo, Moo."

At four o'clock Billie rang the bell, and announced that the bar was closing. But it was forty-five minutes later, during which he and Lewis had another drink or two, that he finally turned out the lights. The three of us closed the place and staggered along the boulevard in the early light to the Dôme. A beggar emerged from the shadows. One of the sleeves of his jacket hung loose. Lewis assumed that he was pretending he had lost an arm, which he was, and upbraided him at length. Then he gave him some money, tried to kick him as he turned to walk away, lost his balance and would have fallen if I had not caught him. He knocked over some trash cans, tumbling their contents into the street. Then he stopped two men in uniform who were walking down the street.

"You must be writers," he said. "Écritures."

They did not understand.

"I'm un écriture," he said. "Name's Sinclair Lewis. Ever hear of me?"

They shook their heads and walked on. Lewis was incomprehensibly amused by this. "I thought everyone had heard of me," he called after them, and went into gales of laughter.

I spotted a taxi which had just pulled up in front of the Dôme. A drunken American had climbed out, and was attempting to pay the driver, and talking about how beautiful it was in Colorado. I asked the driver if he was free. When he nodded, I urged Lewis to get in. He didn't want to.

"Well, you could come and sleep with me," I said. "My place is just around the corner."

"That's the best offer I've had tonight," Lewis said. "I'll take the cab." I helped him into it and directed the driver to Lewis's hotel, the George V. I watched the cab roll away, hoping that Lewis would get home with his wallet intact. I stood for a moment. The morning was hung with haze. A horse-drawn wine dray drew up before the Dôme to unload. The sidewalk gleamed, washed wet, and birds were beginning to chirp in the quiet leaves of the trees along Montparnasse. The city was waking up, and I was on my way home to bed.

In fact, I wrote Mother that the only thing I disliked about living in that beautiful and exciting city, was that I got so little sleep, mostly because of the American tourist maelstrom which whirled me about. Tourists, I wrote, must be related to owls; they rarely go to bed until dawn.

But then Paris is a playground. What other city has such a number of excellent restaurants, sidewalk cafés, grog shops, art galleries, theatres, parks and such relaxed morals? The sidewalk cafés alone are worth the expense of crossing the Atlantic; they are theatres in which you can sit for hours, sipping liquids and watching the drama of life.

But I get so little sleep that some mornings I get up and see a ghost of myself in the mirror: a gray, thin, weary face that bears the marks of burning the candle at both ends.

I know what you're going to say, and tonight I am going to go to bed early. I am already home, and on my way here I saw a recurring French comedy: a fire. I walked up the boulevard Raspail, and heard a dreary tooting. Then a block away a small red machine hove into view and swung around the corner ahead of me. French fire engines are half automobile and half truck: outside, brass-hatted firemen sit in leather jackets and high boots. I followed a small stream of pedestrians and cyclists around the corner to a smoking cinema. Smoke was billowing from the windows on the second floor; the fire must have started in the projection booth. The fire engine stopped in the middle of the street and the pompiers leaped off and hastily unwound a spool of hose. One of them bustled off with it, apparently on his way to a hydrant. The others stood clustered together, staring transfixed at the smoke, waiting for water to gush from their end of the hose. When nothing happened, they huddled in conference and then one of them went up to the entrance door and smashed it with an axe.

It seemed to me, as it would to any fool, that the door could have been opened by simply turning the knob. The axer came back and the firemen once more stood together and surveyed the scene, which now included tongues of flame amid the smoke.

Another fire engine came tooting up and the new pompiers unrolled the hose and went through the same motions as the first group. They all joined together and had another conference. Presently a car drove up and a man emerged, wearing a brass hat and spats, and carrying a staff of authority. Apparently he was the fire chief. On his instructions two of the pompiers opened the smashed door and entered the burning building. By now we were part of a large crowd. A gendarme had come on the scene and was very busy telling us where to stand and so on. After a few minutes the two firemen came running out of the building. There was still no water coming from the hoses. A window shattered on the second floor: glass rained down, and flames shot out.

After a while, when water still had not appeared, I got tired and went home. I imagine that building is a pile of cinders by now.

XV
A Passionate Interlude
and Shakespeare & Co.

I had met Lacy Kastner when Charlie Chaplin came to town. After Chaplin left, Lacy and I and Lacy's wife Priscilla became close friends. He was European head of United Artists and several years older than I. But we had some things in common. They invited me to their attractive house in Neuilly whenever they needed an extra man. I met a lot of famous people through them—most of them connected with the film world.

One day Priscilla called and invited me to dinner. "I have a lady I want you to meet," she said. "Her name is Nan Sunderland. She's an actress, she's on a round-the-world trip, and she's going to marry Walter Huston."

"Who?"

"Walter Huston. The actor."

I remembered that name. I had heard it first from Huston's first wife Rhea at the time when she had gone into raptures over the talents of her son John.

Nan Sunderland was a beautiful woman. She was tall—about five feet nine—with auburn hair, brown eyes, and a sprinkling of freckles on her nose. And I thought she was very nice, as well.

"I hear that you're an actress," I said. "And that you're going to be married to an actor. As a matter of fact I met his first wife." I told her about Rhea.

"I've never encountered so much maternal idolatry in my life," I said. "I don't believe anybody could be as gifted as she says John is. Do you know him?"

"I've met him. He's charming. But you're right. His mother really lays it on thick."

The four other guests that night were two owners of French theatres and their wives. It was a pleasant evening: as always, the food was delicious, the service excellent and the wines superb. When the other guests had left, Lacy asked me to escort Nan back to her hotel. "It's on the rue Jacob, near St Germain de Prés. On your way home."

"I wouldn't care if it was in Deauville," I said gallantly. "I'd consider it a privilege."

"Don't forget, she's engaged to be married."

Lacy summoned a taxi and soon after we were on our way, Nan, to my utter surprise, suddenly turned my face with her hands and kissed me. "There," she said, "that's for taking me home."

I was nonplussed, elated, aroused and emboldened. "I can't fly on one kiss. I must have at least two," I said. We kissed again, more fervently this time. "How long are you going to be here?"

"I really don't know. Walter is divorcing his second wife and doesn't want me to come back to California until that is settled. They were in vaudeville together, and now that he has become so successul in the movies she doesn't want to let him go. If she knew I was waiting in the wings, she'd demand more money."

Nan in costume

"While you're here, you'll need an escort. I apply for the job."

"I'd love it," she said and pecked me demurely on the cheek. "I need some company. I've been by myself for almost four months, ever since I sailed from California."

"You sound like a sailor who returns after months at sea."

"It's been like that." She laughed nervously and took my hand in both of hers. "We'll just be friends," she said, "have fun together. After all, I'm going to be married."

"I'll try," I said. "But it's not going to be easy."

"I know," she said.

And it wasn't easy. Passion kept popping up, testing our moral strength. Wine weakened us, too. During her stay in Paris I saw her almost every day. We went here, there and everywhere together, making a concerted effort to keep our relationship platonic.

But there was a fervent, intoxicating magnetism between us, proving to be a powerful force. When we were alone in my apartment or her hotel room, at the right time it would have been a small miracle if we had been able to restrain ourselves. She was far away from her fiancé, and our relationship cast no reflection on her betrothal. She had had other sexual encounters. She had not promised to be chaste, although she would promise later during the marriage ceremony. I, of course, was free to do as I pleased. Thus we had a rare and wonderful opportunity to enjoy a brief fling, to toss aside inhibitions and obey the urge of nature without hurting anyone. It was natural and buoyant.

We never discussed the rightness, the propriety of our affair. I don't think Nan ever felt any guilt; I certainly didn't. We were healthy, sophisticated adults and, feeling about each other as we did, keenly aware that we had but a short time to be together, we would have been saints not to have succumbed to the blissful conjugation.

I wrote to Mother about her:

> She is a marvelous companion. She was born in Fresno, California, where her father once was mayor. She goes to the Alliance Française to learn French every day while I work. When I am free we touch the bases and the high spots. I'm not getting much of my own work done: *Men Are April When They Woo* is suffering. But I am doing a lot of wooing—knowing that I'm second fiddle and my time for performance is short. We visit art galleries, theatres, one-star restaurants and we sit on cafe terraces and watch the world go by. Fortunately she insists on sharing the expenses—otherwise I'd be in the poorhouse or in jail.
>
> She's interested in the literary scene. We ran into Ford Madox Ford and Ludwig Lewisohn at the Dôme, and I introduced her to them. She was so impressed that she bought a book by each of them: Ford's *No Enemy*, which is autobiographical, and Lewisohn's *The Island Within.*
>
> She likes Sparrow Robertson's column even though Sparrow's writing is anything but literary. So I introduced her to him. Eugene O'Neill is one of Sparrow's pals. So when he came in town from his place in Cap d'Ail we met him. Since she is an actress, she was awed and overjoyed to meet him. Sparrow invited us to join him and O'Neill at the Select on the Champs Élysées. Nan asked O'Neill about *Mourning Becomes Electra,* which I believe is still playing in New York. I don't know whether you've seen it. It lasts for five hours. O'Neill said he wished he had written it as a novel. His next play, he said, is called *Ah, Wilderness* and will open in New York this

winter. It's about a boy coming into manhood, and it's a comedy. This surprised me, because he seems so shy and melancholy. I can't imagine him writing a comedy.

Nan bought a copy of *Electra* and she and I read parts that evening. We were both rather disappointed. But I suppose it's not fair to judge a play on paper, without actors or a set. We thought it was depressing, and the incest upset us. I like O'Neill's earlier, realistic plays: *The Long Voyage Home, The Moon of the Carribbees* and *Beyond the Horizon.* Those are his best, I think. Like Chaplin's early films. But since O'Neill and Chaplin have become famous, they seem anxious to seize art by the throat to choke dollars from it. I'm not saying that money is all they are interested in. That would be stupid. But they have come to take themselves too seriously. They want to do stupendous things, to paint the largest canvas ever painted, or write the longest play ever written, or hoe a row further than anyone ever hoed before. I suppose it's natural. I guess everyone wants to be remembered forever for something.

Now that I have given you my opinion of "America's greatest living playwright", I am announcing that my next work will be a play entitled *Queen Macabre.* I'm basing it on the Snyder-Gray murders I covered in New York. Maybe it will open the door to undying fame for me. (That's a joke.)

I didn't want Nan to miss going to Shakespeare and Co., the famous bookstore on the rue de l'Odéon, not far from the Deux Magots. Sylvia Beach, who owned it, was a small, intelligent, friendly woman. She was the daughter and granddaughter of ministers, but there was nothing pious about her. She dressed in masculine clothes, wore no make up and just ran a comb through her hair. The walls of her shop were decorated with photographs of

Sylvia Beach

writers she had befriended and she had a large fishbowl filled with goldfish, each of which had a pet name. When I brought Nan there, Sylvia took us in the back to the parlor where her literary friends got together. Today it was deserted. It had a fireplace and comfortable chairs. Manuscripts by Walt Whitman were on permanent display.

Sylvia served us tea, and told us how she had come to publish *Ulysses*. "Joyce always had difficulty getting his work published," she said. "When finally *The Little Review* in New York began to publish it in segments, he was overjoyed. And then of course the censors descended. He was heartbroken. I felt so sorry for him. In a wild moment I suggested I publish the entire manuscript as a book. Oh, what a job! I didn't know what I was getting into. Joyce is the most demanding of authors. His proof revisions and corrections drove the French printers mad. It took almost a year to produce the book—and I have to tell you that it is riddled with typographical errors."

The first edition ran to nine hundred pages, printed on cheap paper. It sold for sixty francs, a very high price for a book in France but it sold well from the beginning. All the Right Bank bookstores carried it, as well as Shakespeare and Co. That summer tourists by the hundred bought it for what they all considered its "obscene" passages and smuggled it home. It was banned in both England and the U.S.A.

Because of it Sylvia became known as a publisher of erotica. Writers with questionable work came to her—among them D.H. Lawrence with *Lady Chatterly's Lover* and Frank Harris with *My Life and Loves*. She turned them all down.

Sylvia told us about other Americans who, because of the success of *Ulysses*, decided to take a stab at publishing. Many American, British and Irish writers had come to Paris after the World War, anxious to break away from Victorian and Edwardian conventions. They were looking for ways to find an audience. Robert McAlmon, who was himself a promising writer, started *Contact* editions to publish his work and the work of other unknown writers whom he admired. His money came from his father-in-law. He published some of the early work of William Carlos Williams and Ernest Hemingway, and his *Contact* magazine printed work by, among others, Nathaniel West, Erskine Caldwell, S.J. Perelman and Ivor Winters. Other publishers were Bill Bird, with his Three Mountains Press, Edward Titus with Black Manikin Press, Nancy Cunard and her Hours Press, and Caresse and Harry Crosby and their Black Sun Press. They all gave exposure to struggling writers, using money which they themselves had not earned. They were by and large dilettantes, and of course they promoted themselves at the same time as they helped the writers. The collapse of 1929 jerked the presses from under them.

Priscilla and Lacy Kastner invited Nan and me to lunch with them in a restaurant outside Paris. They picked us up at the Select near the *Herald* offices in a large, chauffeur-driven limousine. With them were Gordon and Mary Ellen Pollock. Gordon, tall and classically handsome, with curly white hair and vivid blue eyes, was an outstanding cinematographer who was in Europe to supervise a film being made by United Artists. His wife, a short woman without his physical beauty, had come along for the ride.

It was a beautiful day, and we were all in a good mood. We sang as we rode along: "The Marseillaise," "My Country 'Tis of Thee," "The Dutch Company." The chauffeur was very sober. He was small and thin, wore a necktie, a jacket and a visored cap, and horn-rimmed glasses on his pale, clean-shaven face. Nan whispered that she did not believe he was really a man. This gave rise to much amusement.

The restaurant was a remodeled ancient mill, thirty miles beyond the perimeter of Paris. It had been built as a mill in 1244 and restoration had turned it into one of the most attractive and luxurious restaurants in the country. We sat at a table under a huge elm at the fork of two brooks. Before lunch was served, Nan and I got into a rowboat and floated down the stream's main artery, sipping aperitifs. We turned back because of the current and I excused myself to go to the W.C.

While I was in there the chauffeur entered. I paid little attention to him but, as I was buttoning my fly, the sound of water running distracted me. I looked up to see the chauffeur squatting over the holes in the floor which served as toilets.

"Je suis une femme," the driver said.

Taken aback, I bowed and said, "How do you do?"

She smiled. "Merci," she said.

I knew it was time for me to leave. "Au revoir," I said. "Bon apetit."

I returned to the table, rather shaken. After a sumptuous lunch and while we were taking benedictine and coffee, I said, "Guess what. Our chauffeur is a female."

"I told you so," Nan said. "How did you find out?"

I told them about the recent scene. Lacy still did not believe me. On the ride back home I asked the chauffeur to tell them. "Je suis une femme," she repeated. She said she dressed like a man because it was dangerous for a woman to drive a taxi, particularly at night. She came from Nice; her child was living there with her grandmother. She had been separated from her husband for five years. She worked as many as sixteen hours a day, seven days a week, saving her money so that she could go back to Nice and open a bistro. Lacy hinted that perhaps she could earn more money in an older profession?

She was not offended. She laughed and said she was a one-man woman.

"My sentiments exactly," Mary Ellen said. It was obvious she idolized her handsome husband.

I saw the Pollocks several times in Paris and got to know them well later when we all lived in California. Their marriage was disturbingly one-sided. Gordon was a philanderer. He used his attractiveness to women to behave like a sheik or a caliph with a harem, choosing at will. Mary Ellen knew about his promiscuity; she was so happy to be his wife that she never protested it. She felt flattered that he treated her with casual affection.

She reminded me of Nora, James Joyce's wife. She too lived with a man who was the object of idolatry. Although Joyce was not a roué, he gave her little of his time, immersing himself in his work while she looked after him and gave him all her affection. All she received in return, it seemed to me, was the right to bask in the background of his fame.

XVI
Art Criticism and a Visit to Fontainebleau

Nan left Paris to go to England for a fortnight's visit to some rich friends. The night before, we went to the Comedie Française to watch a comedy on the most popular theme for farces in that theatre: cuckoldry. Husbands were dupes, wives duplicitous, and paramours satyrs. The audience took part in the performance as they often do, shouting approval or disapproval and adding to the general merriment. The next morning she left for Eastbourne, on the channel south of London where her hosts, who owned several legitimate theatres in London, had a beach house. She promised to write, and a few days later I got a letter:

> Eastbourne is a beach town and I am in a palatial residence that reminds me of the Newport mansions I've seen in *Vogue*. There are many imposing houses here. The middle class, I believe, go to Brighton, some miles down the coast.

People swim in the Channel but I don't. It's too cold and when the tide is out you have to walk half a mile. I am being entertained royally. My only difficulty—apart from my California accent—is with the servants. There are so many that I have a hard time remembering not only their names but their faces and what they are supposed to do. The pecking order among them is as precise as among the aristocracy. The procedure as I understand it (and please don't quote me) is to tell the head butler to tell the second butler to tell the first maid to tell the chambermaid to lay out my clothes for dinner.

I'm catching on, but so far I've been doing it myself and I'm sure the servants consider me common, which, being American, of course I am. Servants are convenient, but I don't think I could live with this many. No privacy. I'm keeping it quiet, but between thee and me, I'll be glad to get back to Paris where I have only one servant: you.

I wrote to Mother:

I have just received word from Jean Wick that *Gun Girl* is to be published next week (probably by the time you receive this letter). Please hasten to Brentano's and ask to buy a copy. If they don't have it, tell them to order it. I am chasing down every connection I can think of to get reviews. This business of becoming famous takes a lot of work and has its drawbacks.

About *Men Are April,* Miss Wick writes, 'It is more finished than *Gun Girl,* with a bigger canvas and better characterization. But I am afraid it will not appeal to the great book-buying public. Personally, I do not like this type of book, and I did not have a good time reading it. But I think it's worthwhile and I'm sure we'll be able to sell it.'

I think Miss Wick disliked my protagonist who is always chasing girls. I think she disapproved of the sex scenes. I imagine McBride will dislike it too. Meanwhile I am working on *Queen Macabre,* but just enough to keep my hand from getting rusty.

You may remember my mentioning a minister, Elmer Long, from Bucyrus, Ohio, whom I met when I was in the hospital. He was an alcoholic but an American girl here cured him, and they have gone back to the States. They are going to start a new church there.

Nan Sunderland is in England visiting friends and is due back this week.

Nan's train got in before noon. I had to go to the American Club luncheon, a weekly assignment, so I met her at the station and took her with me. The Club's members were managers of Paris branches of American companies, attachés at the Embassy and Consulate, doctors, lawyers, retired-from-the-money-race expatriates and at least one artist. As a group they could double for any Rotary or Kiwanis Club membership anywhere in the States. They met every Thursday in a hall on the Champs Élysées and after lunch they listened to a speech. During my time I heard addresses by Charles Lindbergh, Charlie Chaplin, Samuel A. Rothafel, James J. Walker, Andre Tardieu, Adolph Ochs, and Hendrik Van Loon. On this particular Thursday, no visiting celebrities were available, so the Club dipped into its own roster.

The speaker was an artist named Willoughby McElroy Sims, a well-known boulevardier who looked like an artist in the comic strips: his long stringy graying hair flowed down his back, he had an abundant moustache, and he wore a broad-brimmed black hat, a black cape and a perpetual scowl.

His subject today was modern art. He loathed it. He focused his talk on Picasso, then in his cubist phase: he painted nudes in varicolored bits, so that they looked like a scrambled puzzle.

"He galvanizes the female figure, nature's finest work, into terrifying action, distorting it into caricature," Sims said. "He calls it his metamorphosis style. The word means transforming by magic or withcraft. Now what has magic and witchcraft got to do with painting? Absolutely nothing. Like most modern art, it is nonsense.

"If art is one of the great values of mankind, it should reach into the spirit; it should teach magnanimity, humility, tolerance and wisdom. If that is true, and I strongly believe it is, so-called modern artists are off the mark. Picasso's cubistic figures are repugnant; all they do is reach into your spleen. There is no question about his imagination, but what pleases him does not please me. I think what pleases him is the publicity he gets for his strange ideas. Even lousy art, if publicized widely, will sell.

"But I suspect Picasso is painting with tongue in cheek, that he is playing a practical joke on the art world, a canard. Canard is a French word meaning duck, which, because of an old joke, has come to mean hoax. The joke is about a man who owned twenty ducks. They were hungry but he had nothing to feed them so he cut up one of them and fed it to the others. He continued this procedure until there was only one duck left. And that one he ate himself.

"I think Picasso should paint a picture of the man and his ducks, because it seems to me that he regards all of life as a practical joke. After that, because he is such a libertine, I think he might do well to confine his painting to the fleur de lis. At least the pictures would be pretty and perhaps we could understand them."

The audience enjoyed the speech. Encouraged, he went on to denounce art critics, saying they reminded him of people who wrote about wine. "They use esoteric words and phrases with obscure meanings trying to give depth to feeling and taste. They search their minds for remote images and murky scenes to describe an artist's work. They delve into the metaworld and the sixth dimension and dredge up isms to describe what they find. Someone dreamed up the word 'dadaism' for example, to describe the work of artists who use the incongruous and accidental. Not bad. But what such writers are trying to do, it seems to me, is impress the reader with their own erudition. . ."

When the speech had ended and we were outside, Nan said, "I don't agree with him about Picasso. I don't wholly understand Picasso, but I think he has a lot of style. But I do agree with Sims about art critics. Most of them are really hard to understand: as opaque as nocturnes."

We parted so that I could go up to my office and write up the speech. Going toward the Arc de Triomphe, sunlight flickered through the yellowing leaves of the trees bordering the Champs Élysées. Ladies promenaded the wide walk with poodles; nurses wheeled baby carriages. Two little girls in frilly dresses, holding balloons by strings, skipped past me. I passed old men sitting on benches admiring the ladies. It was a familiar scene. Suddenly I felt touched by it more deeply than usual because I knew I was going to leave it. I had been in Paris for almost five years, and recently I had felt an urge growing to move on. Nan's leaving was undoubtedly a factor. But mostly I felt as though I had passed a watershed, now that my first book had been published. I wanted to pursue a literary career full-time.

At Rond Point I had to wait for the traffic to subside.

Even though the desultory gendarme waved his white baton, the cars streamed on, the drivers oblivious to him. Finally a timorous woman stopped her car at the policeman's signal and those behind her were forced to follow her example. So we pedestrians were able to cross.

Where would I go? What would I do? I couldn't just go somewhere, hole up in a room and work away. I had to eat from time to time. I could not afford to go to the south of France, which had been my first plan. I loved Paris, but I felt it was time to return to New York where I could contact book and magazine publishers and editors. I was a great believer in personal contact. I needed a Guggenheim Fellowship or an advance on royalties. I could get along on a hundred dollars a month, maybe even seventy-five. . .

Because Sims' statements were controversial, my story ran on page one. As a result the paper got a lot of letters to the editor. Elliot Paul was delighted, because he often had to spend a lot of time writing these letters himself. More than half the letters praised Sims and agreed with him. The other half were from artists and art dealers. There was one from Picasso himself. He wrote in English: "Tell that ignorant son-of-a-bitch Sims he doesn't know what he's talking about."

A few evenings later, I entered the Deux Magots to meet Nan. She was waiting at the table, and handed me a cablegram. "It's come," she said. I unfolded it.

"Coast is clear. Come home. Love and hurry. Walter."

I handed it back to her with a false smile. "Congratulations," I said, trying to sound sincere. "You warned me it was inevitable."

"It's been a long time coming."

"I know it makes you happy. I'm really glad for you. When do you leave?"

"I've been scurrying around all day trying to make arrangements. I leave day after tomorrow for Marseilles and I sail Thursday to New York on the *President Garfield.* The Dollar Line. Then it's off to California on the train."

The garçon came up. "We'll have to celebrate," I said, sighing. "What'll you have?"

I ordered two gins. "We still have one day and it's my day off," I said. "If you can spare the time from packing, let's make the most of it. Let's go out into the country, to Fontainbleau."

"Good, I'd like that. I can have a last look at the sunshine and the brook."

When the drinks came, we clinked glasses on my toast: "To the end of one romance and the beginning of another."

She said a little later, "But this is not the end of our friendship. You'll be coming to Hollywood. You're going to sell your book to the movies."

"You sound like an oracle," I said. "I hope you're right."

"Ask your mother." She laughed. "She's the fortune teller."

We had dinner that night at Lipp's and then went to the Viking so that Nan could say goodbye to Billie. It was almost eleven o'clock when we got there and as usual at that hour the place was crowded. Voices, laughter, clicking of glasses, rustle of moving bodies fused with the smell of tobacco, alcohol, licorice and olives. We had come in only for one drink and a goodbye. We sat at a table with a young man and woman with pronounced upper-class English accents who had apparently been drinking for some time.

They ignored us and continued their conversation. "Oh, no, Carlton," the young woman was saying. "It's much more difficult to ride sidesaddle. I ride sidesaddle, so I think I should know. I've been riding sidesaddle since I was a child. I can jump or do anything sidesaddle.

"Sissified," the young man said.

"Sissified! Don't be absurd. It's damned difficult. You have to throw your leg over the pommel like this." She pushed back her chair and demonstrated in her skirts. "And bring it down tight against your left." She uncrossed her legs and pulled her chair closer to the table. "Damned hard to do sitting on a horse."

"Old women," the young man said. "Old women ride sidesaddle."

"That's nonsense," she said. "You've got to know how. You've got to go up with the horse, to help him. You lean to the right instinctively when you ride sidesaddle, but when you jump, you must keep dead center. It's damned hard."

"Doesn't look easy. Looks awkward, damned awkward."

"If you don't know what you're looking at. You can't fool a horse, you know." She looked at us suddenly, and met our eyes. "Come on, Carlton," she said abruptly. "It's time to go."

They left, still arguing.

Billie, who had been busy behind the bar, came up to us after a while, his cherubic face beaming. "Our beautiful friend here is leaving," I said. "Going back to California to be married."

"I came to say goodbye," Nan said.

"Well, well, do tell! This calls for a celebration!"

He fetched a chilled bottle of white wine and three glasses. He filled the glasses and raised his, saying, "This is the hardest part of life in Paris, bidding goodbye to good friends. I wish you bon voyage. God bless you. May your marriage be a happy one."

We drank to that.

"Billie," I said, "you're British, aren't you?"

"Welsh."

"Do you ride?"

"Used to, when I was a toddler."

"Ever ride sidesaddle?"

"Heavens, no," he said, laughing. "Only women ride sidesaddle."

"We've just had a lesson on it from a young woman who was sitting at this table."

"Oh, yes, I know who you mean. She's the daughter of Lord and Lady Londesborough. Very good horsewoman. She was in the Olympics, you know. I used to work for her family."

Someone called him. He kissed Nan goodbye, on the cheek, and went off. Nan and I finished the bottle and then left.

The next morning we took a train to Fontainbleau and rented bicycles near the railroad station to pedal our way to Barbizon, the art colony, some twenty kilometers away. We were not sure of the route, and there were no signs on the road. Twice we stopped at farmhouses to get directions.

It was one of those rare poetic days, with a clear sky and the air was warm but without humidity. It was the kind of day that lifts the spirits and quickens the heart. We rolled along laughing and singing, enjoying every minute of the last act of this delightful romance that seemed as though it could go on this way forever. I felt like a doomed man enjoying his last meal, savoring every bite of caviar, lobster and truffles.

We seemed to get to Barbizon awfully fast. It was a sleepy, picturesque hamlet with one main street. We visited Millet's studio with its windows covered with cotton curtains, left just as it had been when he died. We looked at the fields where he had painted "The Gleaners," "The Sower" and "The Angelus." We visited Theodore Rousseau's house as well. It was grander than Millet's, but it moved us emotionally. On that one street was also the small hotel where Robert Louis Stevenson had written *Road Notes.* We lunched there.

After coffee and eau-de-vie we started back to Fontainebleau. Our waitress had told us about a shorter route which, to our delight, led through a dense forest of magnificent trees, the leaves of which obscured the sky. Under our feet was a soft carpet of moss. By that time we were sleepy, so we paused there for a chat. The silence in the forest was overwhelming. After a while we fell silent. We lay on the moss and listened to the musical breezes in the trees. Words began to seem obtrusive. The silence seemed sacrosanct. We lay on our backs, Nan's head was on my shoulder. "'Farewell, farewell,'" I said, quoting from an old poem. "'a lonely sound that always brings a sigh.'" Then I added a touch of Byron: "I only know we did not love in vain."

"Nothing is lost," Nan said. "You said you believe that the sounds of all the ages are out there somewhere, in the heavens."

"That's right. And as long as we are alive, we'll have the memories."

That evening we dined with the Kastners. I took Nan back to her hotel early so that she could finish last-minute packing and get a good night's rest.

Early the next morning we went together to the depot. Everything had been said. So our words were perfunctory. It was a relief to both of us when the whistle sounded the train's departure. We hugged clumsily and kissed for the last time. We were lovers no longer. Suddenly, like the closing of a book, she belonged to someone else. "God speed," I said. "Until we meet again."

"Make it soon," Nan said.

She followed me out to the vestibule. I went down onto the platform and we were still smiling at each other when the train began to move. I stood and watched it disappear.

XVII
A Round of Farewells

I wrote to Mother that I now had time to work on my play because Nan had left.

> I gave her your address and she promised to look you up. I hope to finish this thing in about a month; the first draft is almost completed. Nan helped me. God knows I needed all the professional help I could get, since I never had written anything for the theater before. There is an advantage writing plays has over writing novels: plays only cover about 150 pages. *Men Are April* runs about 400.
>
> In your last letter you said you would check my chart to ascertain my future, which seems very uncertain just now. I've been holding my breath until I hear from you. Nan said she thought I could sell *Gun Girl* to the movies. Please shine up your crystal ball and let me know whether I'm going to remain here, or remove myself, whether I should sell grand-mother's gold watch and buy a ticket to New York or continue stealing bananas from the corner fruit stand.

I had dinner tonight with Eugene Rosetti. He
works as a tipster for the *Herald*. He's a stout, balding
but hairy Rumanian who wears a black derby even
when he's eating. He was in the Rumanian secret service during the War. He used to be a royalist but now
he's a communist. Anyway he knows a lot about
what's going on in Europe and he's an interesting,
stimulating character. I bring him up because he told
me a sensational story which I want to pass on to you.

The story was about Hitler. I had asked Rosetti
whether he knew anything about him.

"Sure," he said. "I know a lot about him. Germany is in
chaos, people are poor and unemployed, and the choice
there is between Hitler and the communists. It's because
of Hitler that I've become a communist. Communism is
the better by far. Hitler hates Jews and Slavs, of which I
am one. He's a crackpot. He believes in the racial superior-
ity of Aryans, whatever that means. He wants Germany to
withdraw from the League of Nations, to repudiate the
Lucarno Treaty and to take over the Rhineland. That
could mean war, you know."

"I know all that," I said. "Everyone does. I've read all
that. But what about him, himself? What kind of person is
he?"

"He's a psychopath, a sexual pervert. And I know
something else about him. He's a murderer. He killed his
niece, and he got away with it."

"How do you know that?"

"I got it from a doctor who treated him psychologi-
cally for sexual problems. I don't think Hitler has made up
his mind what he is, sexually. His tastes run to aberrations. His niece's name was Grete, Hitler called her Geli.
She was only fifteen. Her mother was his half-sister; she
brought the child to live with Hitler in Munich. He tried to

seduce her and when she refused him he would not let
her out of the house. Eventually she submitted to being
molested. This was a form of molestation that included
whipping, you know. Eventually she became so dis-
tressed that she tried to escape, to tell the police. There
was a violent quarrel. He shot her."

"And he got away with it?"

"They held an inquest in Munich. The prosecutor
wanted to charge him with murder, but the Minister of
Justice of Bavaria said the girl had committed suicide,
which is what Hitler claimed. He dismissed the case."

"Even if it were suicide, he would still have driven her
to it," I said.

"Precisely. And this monster is trying to become
Chancellor of Germany! Fortunately the Chancellor must
be appointed by the President, and I don't think Hinden-
burg will do it. But if he does, God help the Germans."

"God help us all," I said.

Another thing I got from Rosetti, which I sent my
mother, was his recipe for the world's greatest salad
dressing. He called it Albert—perhaps in honor of some
Rumanian prince. He started by smearing the bowl with
fresh garlic. Then he mashed a hard-boiled egg yoke and
some English mustard into a powder, added salt, pepper,
oregano, wine vinegar and olive oil and mixed them all
well together. His last gesture was to dip in a finger and
taste it. If it didn't meet his standards he added a little
more this and a little more that.

The day after I wrote this letter, the *Bremen* docked at
Cherbourg, bringing me a letter from Jean Wick. It was in
my box at the *Herald* when I arrived for work. I opened it
eagerly. The impact of what I read was strong enough to
send me slumping to a sitting position on the floor. I
could hardly believe my eyes. A dream had come true.

She had enclosed a check for $300, and there were other surprises: McBride had accepted *Men Are April When They Woo* and Jean had gotten me a contract to write a scenario for Columbia Pictures.

"They want you to do one about a stunt man," she wrote. "For you that should be easy. I told them you'd report for work as soon as you could get there, perhaps a month from the time you receive this. Salary $200 a week."

Stunned, I read the letter again and looked closely at the check. I didn't know whether to cry like a baby or shriek like a banshee. Vince Bugeja was sitting closest to me; he got up and came to my assistance.

"Are you all right, old fellow?" he asked, solicitously.

I got up slowly, rubbing my buttocks. I'm not sure," I said. "I'm stultified, paralyzed and benumbed."

"I thought you'd had a heart attack."

Booj was an attractive, dark-skinned Maltese with curly black hair. He had graduated from Cambridge with a first, had been a Jesuit briefly, was internationally known as a photographer, spoke several languages fluently, including Arabic, had an independent income and was something of a playboy. He had come into the *Herald* offices looking for a job. He said he had no experience but he had been reading the paper and he thought he could do a better job with it than the writers already employed. Oddly enough, he was hired. He did do well. And after that he took over the editorship of the organ of the Maltese Labor Party and ran it from Paris while he continued editing the *Herald*. He also became head of the political action committee of the Malta Labor Party.

I addressed everyone in the office. "Hey," I yelled, "listen to this." I read them Jean's letter.

Tom Cope, at the copy desk, said, "Well, bless my soul and body. How lucky can you get?"

Spencer Bull, from the city desk, said, "What's today? April Fool?"

"It's the gospel," I said. "I'm going back to Hollywood! Gonna make some money! It's ironical: when I was there before I tried my best to get any kind of a job in a scenario department, even sweeping out. No one would have me."

After I had shaken everyone's hand, I went across the hall into Eric Hawkins' office. "At last you're rid of me," I said, handing him the letter. His eyes widened as he read it. "Congratulations," he said. "I must say I'm not all that surprised. I've seen a number of people leave this office on their way up the ladder."

He was thinking of Ralph Barnes, who had gone on to head the *Herald-Tribune* burean in Rome; of Al Laney who had gone to the *New York Times* and would write a history of the *Herald;* of Martha Foley and Whit Burnett, who founded and edited *Story* magazine; of Reggie Coggeshall, Jack Pickering, Dean Jennings, Ed Skinner, Bert Andrews, John Watson, George Buchanan, Jack Blalock, Wolfe Kaufman and other excellent editors and reporters who had gone on to more profitable and prestigious careers elsewhere.

"I'll stay another week," I said. "And give you a chance to get a replacement."

He wished me good luck. To take my place he hired Ned Calmer, who went on to become a national radio commentator in the States.

The day before my departure I went to say goodbye to James Joyce. As usual he was at work in his cluttered study where he spent endless hours. He was pale because he rarely went out into the sun. He did not like interruptions, but he greeted me amiably.

"Going to write for the movies," he said. "That should be interesting."

"I'm going to adapt *Ulysses* to the screen," I said, in jest.

"Oh, my God!"

"I hope your work is going well?"

"Slowly, po'ly," he said, giving the second word a black southern pronunciation. This kind of repetition was typical of him. He did not like to talk about his actual work in progress. But he was always willing to discuss his methods of operation. He often said he was the most laborious writer who ever lived; that he spent hours on research, reading and making notes from books and periodicals published in several languages. "I go slowly because writing does not come easily to me," he said. But of course he had to go slowly because of his poor eyesight, which caused him great suffering. After each of his several eye operations he was in despair, because he was afraid he would not be able to write again. For him that would have been like dying.

I thanked him for his many kindnesses, which included allowing me to learn from him.

He asked me what I had learned.

"Well, for one thing, to explore and concentrate on the unusual. To avoid the trite. To work assiduously."

"I hope you have also learned to school yourself against discouragement. As long as you're alive there is no failure."

I shook his boney hand with its long fingers, and mentioned that my agent had suggested I write an article about him, his home life and his working methods for an American magazine. "She tells me there is a lot of curiosity about you," I said.

He put his hand on my arm. "I beg you not to do it," he

Ford Madox Ford

said. "Please. I don't want that kind of publicity. I've often been approached by people from magazines. I always turn them down."

"Well, then of course I won't do it."

"I'm sorry. I suppose you'll lose a large fee."

"Your friendship is more important to me than money."

He asked me for a copy of *Gun Girl*.

I made the rounds, saying goodbye to all my friends: the Kastners, Ford Madox Ford, Alex Calder, Jacques Lip-schitz, Sylvia Beach, and people at the embassy and the consulate, where my closest friend was Robert Murphy, the vice-consul. Bob was working his way up like the rest of us. He had started as a clerk in the U.S. Post office, transferred to the consular service and eventually would be a public figure during World War II when he negoti-ated the Murphy-Weygang accords.

I also bade farewell to my laundress. She was a widow who lived and worked in the back room of a building next to the police station in the rue Delambre. She was a large shapeless woman; her gray wool dress was always damp. She had more work than she could do, so her customers often had to wait. Whenever I brought in my bundle of linen I found her hard at work, breathing heavily. She ate in a restaurant across the street, with the cooks and waiters after the patrons had left. I frequently warned her to go easy on starch and sugar, but of course she paid no attention to me. She had had two children; the boy had been killed in the War, and the girl was living in Casablanca with a black African.

I told her I was going to Hollywood. She thought at first that I was going to be an actor; she was pleasantly im-pressed. But her face fell when I explained I was going to write for movies. "Then," she said in French, "it is very sad."

"No, no," I replied, also in French. "I'll be a writer. I can become rich and famous that way too."

She shrugged and shook her head. I gave her a hundred franc note, and she was overwhelmed with gratitude. She kissed my hand.

My concierge was another middle-aged woman who had always worked like a drudge and never known freedom from care, or real happiness, apparently. During the years I had lived in her house she had kept a sharp, suspicious eye on my affairs, especially when women were involved in them. Her husband was living: he delivered coal and black specks of coal dust were embedded under the skin of his face.

I said goodbye to Alzira and Waldo Pierce in their apartment on the boulevard Raspail. Their twins were now two years old and at home babbling either English or French. I admired their adaptability. "They don't have anything in their heads to confuse them." Waldo said.

The Dôme had been my bailiwick for a long time; it was a deeply engrained part of my life in Paris. I went there and sat on the terrace with a sandwich and a beer. I felt like a butterfly leaving its cocoon. At the very least I was closing the covers of a book.

A small man wearing a wide-brimmed black felt hat, a black suit and a black string tie started across the boulevard toward the Dôme. An aproned man pushing a cart loaded with empty wine bottles almost ran into him. He stopped short, so did the cart, and some wine bottles rolled off the load and smashed on the pavement. At once a heated argument began, complete with insults: Where the hell do you think you're going, you filth-faced dog? Who the hell do you think you are? You think you own the street, you putrid pig? Traffic stopped, an audience gathered. A gendarme strolled over and listened casually. After a while he told the cart-pusher to move along. The cart-pusher complied, still calling insults and the man in black responded energetically. The crowd dispersed, and the road traffic resumed. The man in black, who was an artist, continued on into the cafe. He caught my eye and winked.

These Parisians rarely resort to physical abuse, because in the eyes of the law he who punches first is the guilty one. But the law says nothing about verbal abuse, so hostile energy is expended in thinking up imaginative curses and insults.

A thin mendicant appeared; he had a wire cigarette-holder attached to one of his ears. Without using his hands he could get the cigarette in and out of his mouth, simply by a toss of the head. Fascinated tourists bought these doodads from him for a small sum. He had approached me several times with no success, so he continued on his way without looking at me.

Then a young female teacher came along; she was wearing a broad-brimmed brown felt hat. Behind her trooped a brood of young girls, all the same size, all wearing blue smocks. They reached the corner, the young woman spoke to them, and they all crossed the rue Delambre together. They were followed shortly by two priests carrying missals. They wore black robes and crosses on chains around their necks. They oddly resembled two crows which waddled about behind them, picking tidbits from the street.

I saw Janet Flanner walking by and hailed her. She was on her way to see René Claire and get his ideas on the cinema for one of her articles for the *New Yorker*. She bade me au revoir and good luck.

I had said goodbye to my friends, to the Dôme and to the streets. That evening I set out to bid goodbye to the watering holes. Elliot Paul, George Rehm and Tom Cope came along. We got started around midnight at Harry's New York Bar. From there we went to Henry's and then the Silver Ring. Then we hit Otto's and Johnny's before crossing the river to the Deux Magots, la Coupole and the Viking. By the time I had had a farewell drink or two with Billie at the Viking, we felt hungry and Elliot suggested we go to Les Halles for onion soup.

Les Halles, the central market, was the heart and stomach of the city. It was a tourist attraction almost tantamount to the Louvre. The four of us knew it well, having worked on its fringe before the *Herald* moved to the rue de Berri. We knew the most exciting time to visit it was in the wee hours of the morning when market activity was at its height.

The streets around Les Halles—rue de Louvre, boulevard Sebastopol, and the rue Etienne-Marcel—were clogged with wagons, drays, carts, and bicycles. Huge horses with harnesses and blinders pulled many of the vehicles. Hundreds of people milled about: farmers, clerks, buyers and sightseers. The air was redolent of many different kinds of odors. Among other things, there were mosaics of oranges, carrots, pomegranates, tomatoes, cauliflower, celery, apples, beets, onions, bananas, pineapples, passion fruit, prunes, grapes, melons, nuts, brocolli, eggplant, rhubarb, endive, scallions, squash, zucchini, pimentos, mushrooms, parsley, watercress. . . . There were endless rows of the carcasses of cattle, hogs, and horses, and crates of cooing doves and pigeons, clucking chickens, croaking frogs, quacking ducks, silent turtles, and there was a large section of tubs of flowers.

Our favorite cafe, famous for its onion soup, was Le Jean Bart. Its premises, inside and out, were filled with men and women in blood-smeared smocks, black shirts, aprons and all kinds of headgear. A large back room was reserved for tourists and the neighborhood prostitutes and pimps: it was relatively clean and quiet and more expensive than the rest of the place. We decided to give it a miss, and were able to find a table for four on the sidewalk, where we could see what was going on.

We had two servings of the incredibly good onion soup, along with the world's most delicious fresh bread and strawberry confiture. By the time we finished eating, we were almost sober. The sky behind Notre Dame was growing light; the magnificent cathedral was emerging before our eyes.

"Take a good look," Tom said. "You may never see it again."

Elliot suggested we go into the cathedral. He said it was a good time of day for it.

Inside the light was subdued, provided by flickering candles and the dawn filtered through high stained glass windows. There was the odor of incense, mixed with the odors of wax and dust. The place was pervaded by an impressive spirituality. I found myself praying that I might be allowed to return to Paris.

Someone was listening because I did manage to get back, though it took many years.

Addendum

Addendum

When I got to California, I called Nan, who was now married to Walter Huston and living with him in Beverly Hills. She came to pick me up in a chauffeur-driven limousine and we went to Culver City to get Walter who was working at the time for Metro-Goldwyn-Mayer. It was late afternoon. He had just finished his day's work, and came out of his mobile dressing room with his face shining from the cream he had used to get his make-up off. He smiled and held out his hand to me.

"So," he said, "this is the former stunt man who has returned to the film factories to write screenplays. Welcome back."

I told him I had now met two of his wives. "You've become part of my life," I said. "I feel almost part of your family."

"That calls for a celebration," he said, and we went to the Beverly Hills Brown Derby for dinner.

In time I would learn that I had found a lifelong friend.

But that is another story.

ठ|▽ — BE∅ ÷ E|AB